W9-BPM-893

LaToya's
Life

Uncut Mishaps
of a
YouTube Star

LaToya Ali

To my babies, Samia and Zayn -
I hope my mistakes and achievements
can be referenced in decisions that
you will make throughout your lives.

Table of Contents

"One thing that bothers me in this industry is seeing how much people are willing to give up on their pursuit."

Introduction

hank you for taking the time to open up my book. Who would have thought crazy LaToya would write a book? My goodness, the things you can do if you devote to your idea. Now some of you probably know a lot about me but for those who have never heard of me, I go by LaToya Forever. I am an online personality with a current reach of 2M+ followers. I'm known for my **YouTube** videos and crazy snapchat stories. I love my fans who I refer to as **HUNTYS** (females) and **HUNCLES** (guys) so don't mind me if I start referring to you in the book as a Hunty (honey + auntie). I love to "be happy and make people laugh." That's my motto! I have two amazing children: Samia and Zayn and an annoying husband Adam (Hi Babe, pick up dinner on the way back from the gym you gymrat). All he does is go to the gym and expects me to make 6 meals for his hungry ass. Who has time for that? Anyway, this book wasn't meant to be my personal rant chronicles. I wanted to write a book for this sole purpose: to inspire through my stories. Now let's get this straight-- you can read all the books in the world, attend all the conferences, watch all the videos, and get all the advice.

But if you don't take that single first step to change, nothing will change. I never thought I could change or do anything meaningful in my life. I did have a sense of humor, but I was somewhat reserved and didn't want to do anything that made me look or feel uncomfortable. I'm sure a lot of us would rather go day to day in our comfortable little routine without any sense of being uncomfortable. Shooooot! Can you imagine LaToya writing a book? I am in a new world just writing this right now, but I know in the end I'm going to be happy that I started and that I got to share my journey with readers like yourself. That's what keeps me accountable to go on - MAKING AN IMPACT! That's what we need to find in our lives - a reason WHY we need to do something. That WHY needs to make you CRY (now that's deep). I want to be able to share my story so other people who have goals just like me can also believe they can do whatever they put their mind to and actually charge forward and do it! Sounds cliché and same ol' talk, but I'm telling you I am no different from you.

My goal with you after you complete reading this book is for you to know what is your WHY. At least understand that you will need to eventually find out what that is. A lot of the stories and advice I will be sharing in this book comes from experiences. And as young as I am, I have experienced a lot of good and negative things. One thing I know for sure is that good and bad things will always happen to you, but one thing you will usually have control of is the approach you take in reacting to it. Some of us learn well from people's experiences, and some of us need to experience it our self. I'm a little bit of both, and that's fine if you are too.

What I plan to share in this book isn't some manual on how to live your life or anything. That's already out there. All I hope to do is share experiences that I hope will make you think differently and help you make decisions that you can live with. It's so tough to live a life where everything you do reminds you of a decision you made. That's not living; that's maintaining. Several years ago, I used to go to my retail job during the week, and I would have some clients who would come in and want me to select their outfits. One client of mine, who was a business woman, told me she was so happy because she hit her goal of making $10,000 in a month. She was always open with me, and I could tell she enjoyed her shopping therapy sessions with me. A communication line was definitely there as she didn't hesitate at all in sharing her finances or love battles. Nonetheless, I was shocked that someone could make that kind of money. I quickly asked her: how? And she responded that it all started with a VISION BOARD. I was hoping she would get to the secret of what she does, but all she had for me was VISION BOARD. I googled what a vision board was that night and at first, I was like: WTF? Do things you like on a board help you with actually getting them?

Quickly, I closed my browser window and continued with my day. A couple of weeks went by, and my co-worker came in and told me she got engaged. I congratulated her, and I asked her how she felt. She told me that she was very happy, and she attracted this into her life. That night, I had this light bulb moment that the vision board was a way of attracting things into one's life.

I googled things I wanted to attract into my life. I saved pictures from google images and printed them off and stuck them on a bulletin board I purchased from good ol' Walmart. I had so many things on my vision board like a range rover, a house, an airplane because I've always wanted to travel the world, I had pictures of celebrities I aspire to be like, Beyonce and Tyra Banks. I had bunch of words on there like GRIND, HUSTLE, BE HAPPY, LOVE, CONFIDENCE....

Now, what was on it didn't matter. Looking back 5 years now, all that matters is that everything I had there I attracted into my life. I kid you not!! The mind can do wonders for you if you tap into it. I'm not a motivational speaker (I actually fear public speaking) I'm just telling you what worked for me. We'll get into more about tapping into your mind later in the book.

So let me give you a little breakdown of how it all started —— I was born in Toronto, Canada to Trinidadian parents (TRINI TO DI BONE). My mom was 16 when she was pregnant with me and apparently I was supposed to be aborted. Yep! Aborted!! My mom refused to go that route, and she stuck with me. The reason why abortion was a discussion then was because my Dad (Nigel Wilson) was about to go number one in the 1992 Major League Baseball Draft. He had no business bringing a child into the picture at the age of 17 which would potentially slow down his entrance to the major leagues. My mom quickly shunned everyone who told her to go through with the abortion and she kept me! Before I even hit the world, I was on the verge of death.

My mom brought me to the world, and my Dad was happy to be involved in my life. He's great! However, two teens who barely knew anything about LOVE couldn't withstand the fast pace of life and ended up breaking up early into my life. Thankfully, co-parenting and family helped this little girl grow up to be a wonderful firecracker (like my husband would say).

The Need to Express

rowing up, of course, has its challenges for each and every one of us. Life takes us all through unexpected turns. However, when I look back at my childhood, I can't help but feel like I had it exceptionally hard. I understand that in the grand scheme of things I had a pretty good childhood. But nevertheless, they were my struggles, and they held a lot of weight on me.

I can remember back when I was in grade 8. At that time, I lived with my mom, my stepdad, and my three siblings. My biological dad was a professional baseball player and traveled a lot, so living with him was out of the question. Also, I was a child, and what kid wants to be away from their mom? Mine was ambitious and wanted to continue pursuing a law degree. But to do that we had to move from Ontario, Canada to Tulsa, Oklahoma. This was a lot to take in, and I was caught completely off-guard by the news. I had to pack up and leave everything I knew and loved.

My dad's side of the family was so upset about Mom's sudden decision to move to America to pursue an education.

Why couldn't she just stay in Canada and go to University? My dad's side of the family wanted me to stay and live with them to continue my schooling at the all-girls private school I attended. That side of my family is all about education, so they were livid. My mom and dad had a terrible co-parenting relationship, and they would always argue. I remember Dad talking to Mom on the phone one day. I stood at his door, and all I could hear was: *"Debbie why are you doing this?" "You are going to regret this!" "You are so selfish." "Leave LaToya here."* -- HANGS UP PHONE!

My mom still made the decision to move to Oklahoma and go to the Christian school that she desperately wanted to attend. I remember packing up all of our clothing, and I remember blasting my favorite song: **"You Make Me Wanna"** by Usher. (I was so in love with Usher's music and still am.) The morning after, we packed up the van and we drove off in Mom's all-black Dodge Caravan. My stepdad didn't drive to Oklahoma with us. It was just Mom, my sister, Tani, and my brothers, Shakqueel and PJ. The drive there took nearly 30 hours.

Every time Mom got tired, we would stop at a pit stop and would sleep in the van. I remember Tani and I would tan at the pit stops, and we soaked up all the sun. I remember looking out the window in the passenger seat and thinking to myself, *"I got my Mom's back. Tulsa, here I come."* My brothers were fighting in the back seat the entire trip, and my sister was just rolling her eyes. The drive was so long. I remember fighting sleep because I wanted to make sure my mom was well while driving. I recall driving through Missouri and being very bored because all I saw were bushes, farms, animals, and trees. I asked Mom if Tulsa was that country, and she assured me it wasn't. I wasn't trying to live in farmland. Imagine me living on a farm? Oh hell no!

It was not an ideal situation when we moved because we lived with a random woman that my mom met on some Christian website. Trying to adapt was hard. I remember arriving at Ms. K's house and thinking it was enormous. She lived in a mansion! We were all so excited. I remember at one point asking Mom if it was the right house. We were all so hyped. My brothers were in the back seat saying, "this lady must be rich. Does she have a pool? A basketball court? Are we going to have our own rooms? I remember walking inside, and my Mom introduced us to Ms. K and her son. They gave us a tour of where we would be staying. We had two bedrooms and a bathroom.

> I remember thinking that I wouldn't feel alone, and that I would have someone who understood & could relate to me.

My brothers shared a room, and my mom, my sister and I shared the other room. It was a hot mess, but we made it work. My stepdad didn't come with us right off the bat. He wanted Mom to get a place first before he picked up his entire life to live in Tulsa. In the meantime, we stayed with the lady for several months, and I started to sense that we out-stayed our temporary welcome. Ms. K told my Mom that we had to leave. I could totally understand, housing our entire family rent-free could be taxing to anyone. So we packed up all of our things and we moved into a shelter. We stayed there for a few months, and my Mom was finally approved for a section 8 - 3 bedroom townhouse in the projects. We were all so excited. My stepdad finally moved in with us. My stepdad and I were cool for the most part. My real Dad and I were never close, he had his own family with my three other half-siblings. Can I come clean about something? I feel terrible for feeling this way and I love my siblings, but I've always longed for a full sibling, or better yet a twin. I remember thinking that I wouldn't feel alone, and that I would have someone who understood and could relate to me. This is something I've never really overcome.

I've just gotten stronger and better at dealing with it. When I was back in Canada, it was a little better because I had best friends that I could confide in. But being in Tulsa was completely different. (I was always the new girl, so it was always a chore getting to know new people). I always felt out of place, I always felt like I didn't belong, and people looked at me as an outcast. They called me **"New Girl," "Canada," "Eskimo,"** the list goes on. I hated the fact that I always had to start over. You're probably wondering why I was always the new girl.

Well, we would always move. We were house hoppers, and every time we moved it was out of the school district, which is why I always had to enroll into another school. The reason why we were moving so much is that my mom couldn't afford to pay rent. It was a struggle for her because she was doing it all on her own, no help! I remember one time we moved, and I confronted my mom. Like, how selfish can a person be? She had three young kids, and she really needed to get it together. I hated the fact that my mom couldn't just stay put. It was affecting me emotionally. I would spend endless amounts of time just crying myself to sleep.

I remember I used to pretend to do work in the library during lunch because I had no one to sit with when we ate. This was a tough time in my life, but I was forced just to keep going like anyone would do. Things gradually began to get easier for me. I became more comfortable at school and opened up more until I eventually made some friends.

Things were finally starting to look up. But, as they say, all things come to an end. My home life took another turn when my mom and stepdad split up. One of the main reasons they split up was because he wasn't a US resident, so he couldn't get work. He would try to get under-the-table jobs, or try to start multi-level businesses, and it wasn't working out for him. So he moved back to Canada. It was a sad day for me. My stepdad and I had some great times together. I played soccer, and, honestly, my stepdad was my number 1 fan. He went to all of my soccer games. He would always be on the sidelines yelling. I remember one time one of the girls from the other team tripped me on purpose and my stepdad yelled, **"HELL NO! YOU BETTER TRIP HER BACK."** Everyone on the soccer field died of laughter. When we lived back home in Canada, he was my soccer coach. He was a great father to all of us. He was strict, but he was so awesome. Funny and embarrassing story: I was in the 9th grade, and my stepdad used to drop me off at school. I attended a Christian school at the time. So we pulled up at the school, and right before I opened the door to jump out the car, he opens up the glove compartment and about 20 pairs of thongs fell out. The first thing he said was: **"Why do you have these? Whores wear G-strings. You're grounded."** I was so embarrassed. After that day, my thongs were nowhere to be found. I guess he threw them out. I was so upset that Mom and him split up, but I was secretly ok with it because he was so damn strict. Like, he wouldn't allow me to talk to boys on the phone. I was a teenager for heaven's sake!

But as expected, the split took a toll on my mom...

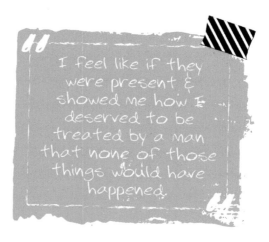

She worked a lot and went to school all the time, so I rarely saw her, and even more seldom would I get advice or comfort from her. When my mom and stepdad split, I saw her even less. She was struggling with the separation, and her way of coping with it was to be around friends. When she wasn't working, she would go out with her friends instead of being with the kids. There were times when she wouldn't come home until the end of the weekend. Since I was the eldest, I was left to watch after my siblings, which made me feel like even less of a sibling to them and more of a caretaker or nanny.

> I feel like if they were present & showed me how I deserved to be treated by a man that none of those things would have happened.

School was going well, so it became my escape where I could not worry about my family situation and just hang out with my friends. I also started becoming interested in boys at this time, and I met a guy who I became really serious about. Being so young and vulnerable is a recipe for disaster. I put a lot of trust in him, and he pushed and pressured me to do things that I didn't want to do. I blame my dad and stepdad for these things. I feel like if they were present and showed me how I deserved to be treated by a man that none of those things would have happened. Or maybe I'm just making an excuse for my own actions - I don't know. They were there for me in different ways.

My biological dad was there for me financially, and my stepdad made me feel like I couldn't talk to him on any topic other than soccer. My boyfriend at the time used to pressure me every day to have sex with him. He would say things like: **"LaToya, everyone is having sex now,"** or, **"Why do you want to wait until you're married? That's old school,"** and, **"Let's just do it. I love you."** I would confide in my friends, and they would tell me just to have sex with him. They told me they were having sex, so it was ok. After all this pressure from my boyfriend and friends, I finally gave in. It hurt so bad, and I did not understand why people raved about it so much. I hated it. I regretted losing my virginity at such a young age. I felt violated, like all my innocence was taken away from me. Looking back, I wish I had been stronger. I wish I had known myself. I wish I could have been strong enough just to say NO to the pressure, but everything happens for a reason. We broke up because I cheated on him with another guy in Tulsa, Oklahoma. One of my friends at the time told my boyfriend, and he broke up with me.

It's worth noting that when we moved to Oklahoma, I was still a Canadian citizen. My mom had her American citizenship, and because I was her child I should have had my American citizenship as well, but that wasn't the case. My mom needed to fill out some required paperwork for me to be an official citizen, but she never got around to doing it (she didn't have the finances). So this posed many difficulties for me, mainly ones around getting a job. I remember I wanted to get a job at 15 years old. I wanted to start making money. I wanted to shop and go to the movies. But not having citizenship prevented me from getting a job. I had no money to my name. Mom felt super bad, and she reassured me that I would get my American citizenship.

" I had the time of my life! "

23

Although, I wish my mom handled my citizenship more seriously, one thing she never let me down was on my 16th birthday... I remember my sophomore year I was turning 16, and my Mom wanted to throw a Sweet 16 Party. I was so happy! My friends and I came together, and we made flyers and gave them out to all the schools I attended in Tulsa. I kid you not: over 300 people showed up. My mom and her best friend were making chicken wings for everyone, we had the music bumping, all my friends were dancing, and my entire house was packed. God blessed our family with a subsidized 2 story home with a spacious backyard, so you know the turn up was real for my Sweet 16. My guests were jamming out on the front lawn, in the house, in the backyard - everywhere! Looking back at this moment, I was very present. I was just living in the moment with all my friends. I remember everyone singing Happy Birthday to me so loud that the entire house was shaking. My birthday cake was so beautiful. My mom came through for me on my Sweet 16. I remember my brother, Shakqueel, trying to dance with one of my best friends; it was the funniest thing ever. I had the time of my life. Thank you, Mommy.

Although my Sweet 16 was fantastic, I still didn't feel complete. I couldn't get my driver's license. Every 16 year-old looks forward to getting their driver's license, so I was super depressed about this. I remember all the cool 16-year-olds whipping around in their cars, and I had nothing. So many of the kids had cars, carpooled or walked home because they lived close. I remember having to take the big yellow school bus. Nobody cool took the big yellow school bus. So I would run to the bus every day after school and lay down in my seat so nobody would see me on the bus as it drove out of the school bus zone. I was that embarrassed. I remember getting into a huge fight with Mom about her preventing me from having a life. I felt like I was missing out on so much as a teenager.

Thinking about my situation, I was so angry that I packed up my things and moved out. I moved to Crystal's house, who was my best friend, for an entire school semester. Looking back, it was actually great. I didn't have to babysit every single day, which forced my mom to get a babysitter, and I didn't have to take the big yellow school bus anymore because my best friend's mom, brother or boyfriend would give us a ride. I remember being left home alone, and Crystal's dog, "Cash" wanted to go outside to pee. So I opened the door, and he ran off. I couldn't keep up. He just ran, and I swear he was going 100mph! I was panicking. When Crystals' mom got home, I told her the news. She went off on Crystal and me. All 3 of us spent at least 4 hours driving around and calling out for Cash. Crystal and I walked the streets for hours every day after school searching for Cash. One random rainy day, Cash showed up. Crystal's mom was so relieved and happy. Thank God Cash came home, because Crystal's mom was not too pleased with me and I was not trying to go back home to take that damn yellow school bus to school.

I got through my Junior year, still angry about not being able to get a job or my license so...

I made the tough decision to move back to Canada to live with my dad. He had retired from baseball, so he didn't travel as much anymore. It was pleasant to be back in Canada and see some of my old friends and family, but living with Dad was a little awkward. Like I said earlier, we weren't close. He also had three other kids with a different woman. I felt out of place living with my dad. I felt like the black sheep of the family. It may sound silly, but small things would make me feel left out. For example, everyone had TVs in their rooms except for me. I remember my dad telling me I had to "earn" a TV...really? While my little sisters and brother had a TV in their room? It was just ridiculous.

Also, my stepmom didn't always see eye-to-eye with me. She would make me clean the house from top to bottom, and if one thing were out of place or not up to her standards, she would freak out on me: *"Umm, LaToya, you're leaving your*

footprints in the house. Can you wear socks?" I look back now, and I laugh at how ridiculous her complaints were. Clearly, she has OCD. I recall my mom and stepmom never seeing eye-to-eye. They got into plenty of arguments. Mom always thought my stepmom was jealous because I was the firstborn. I remember one day I was on the phone with Dad and my stepmom, and my stepmom said I should get a paternity test to prove to my Mom that I'm my Dad's child. She felt like my Mom was promiscuous when she was young. I feel like my stepmom secretly wanted to know for herself because she had doubts about me being my Dad's child. I questioned my dad and my entire family about this, and they called me silly and told me that I was his child. That made me feel better, but back then this thought stayed in the back of my mind. My stepmom put that doubt in me. I'm over it now as I write this, as I know I'm my father's firstborn child. This incident had made my insecurities and feeling of not belonging even stronger. I was lucky enough to have other family members and friends who could assure me that I was my dad's child.

> The positive feedback inspired me to do more & gave me the confidence to put myself out there even more than I already had.

Finding YouTube and Social Media

As a little girl, I was told I had a lot of personality. I was always performing and trying to make people smile and laugh. My mom had a strong belief that I would be in entertainment because my personality was far more than she could handle. One time in high school, I brought tanning spray to my class and I sprayed my teacher's arm because I felt like he needed some sun to improve his mood. Doesn't a nice tan make everyone feel like they've just been on vacation? Plus, I wanted my teacher to look his best. My class thought it was hilarious. My teacher didn't, though. I got two weeks' worth of detention; such a waste of $6.99. I loved making my friends and classmates laugh. They could always count on me to lighten the mood or find a joke in an everyday situation.

Before **YouTube**, there was a platform called BlogTV which was a live streaming platform allowing users to go live on video. This became my outlet to vent my thoughts and socialize with people. As mentioned, I moved around a lot and had to end friendships as soon as they were blossoming. I think this might have triggered my personal need for attention, and **BlogTV** provided that for me. I found joy in getting the attention in the video live shows. I made a name for myself in the community, and I remember people begging me to do shows. I would sing songs and the viewers would laugh hysterically at how bad I sucked.

One time, my Mom had a prayer meeting at the house, and I started live streaming with my brother PJ. So during the live stream he was acting like a ghetto preacher. He would splash holy water everywhere, anoint people's foreheads, and rebuke demons out of people. He pretended to catch the Holy Ghost and just lay there. He would say things like *"I rebuke you in Jesus name" "The Lord said let there be light AAAAAAH and there was light RO BO BO BO SHANDA"* He would speak in tongues. Anyone from a pentecostal church knows exactly what I'm talking about. It was the funniest thing ever! Many viewers loved my show and my crazy fun family. My mom would get pissed at times because I spent all day and all night on BlogTV. It was good times on **BlogTV**.

My very first **YouTube** video was me roaring into the camera like a tiger. I don't know what the hell possessed me to do that, but I did. I got over 1000 views on it. The second video I created was me drinking a bottle of water. I told everyone to drink a bottle of water for good luck, and how water makes me burp. (Please don't judge me, I was so strange.) I was super random on **YouTube** because I was trying to figure out exactly what I wanted to do.

When I think back to my very first video, I am amazed at how far I've come. The only thing I could count on was coming home at the end of the day and turning on the camera to do what I loved. I would do the dumbest, craziest things on camera, and people would just die of laughter. Sometimes I go back and watch those videos just to laugh at myself. I had to put some of these videos on private because I am so embarrassed by them.

Even while I was trying to figure out what I wanted to do with my life, whether it was school or entertaining, I was constantly going

to modeling and casting agencies to try and pursue my dream of being an entertainer. It was hard to get constantly turned down and hear that I wasn't what they were looking for, but I kept at it. I knew that, if I kept trying, one day it would happen for me.

I booked a few little projects, and even now I see my face on a couple of ads here and there. I also had to work to make money because I didn't want to have to depend on my dad. I heard that Hooters paid well, so I decided to pick up a serving job there. It was so fun! Like, I could be myself and no one would judge me because they love when you have a fun and bubbly personality. These attributes are important when engaging with customers who come in to eat and watch sports. I remember this one guy who had the biggest crush on me. Every time he came in, he would bring me jewelry (JEWELRY, people!). It's safe to say I was his favorite Hooters girl, as he always left me decent tips. He was at Hooters every time I had a shift. Hooters was so fun that I remember creating a video on *'How to Become a Hooters Girl,'* and that video got a lot of attention. I got fired from Hooters because I and a couple of the staff got drunk while on a shift. Good times!

I've had countless photo shoots trying to build my portfolio. I had many photographers wanting to work with me to build my portfolio. I used to meet up with photographers and a lot of the time I felt super uncomfortable because they would pressure me to do sexual poses, or wear sexy lingerie. I've had countless terrible experiences with photographers and made decisions I'm not proud of, I look at bad decisions and mistakes I've made as lessons learned. I remember one photographer telling me that I wouldn't make it in the industry unless I had sex with him and how all the models had to have sex with people in the industry to make it to the top! WTF! That really did scare me and I slowly faded away from the modeling agency. Especially because I had associates who thought that was the only way to get to the top. I wanted no part in that. Don't let anyone pressure you into things you don't want to do. What I'm trying to say is, don't feel like you have to do things that go against your values to be something/successful in this world.

One day my friend and I got together and we were thinking of video ideas we could do together. We came up with the idea of creating a parody video. At the time, there was a popular song called *"Hold Yuh"* by Gyptian featuring Nicki Minaj and there was no video for it, so we created a funny video. The video was about a Nigerian man falling in love with a girl wanting to buy her the world, haha. Our video's view count did well, and people seemed to enjoy it. It was our first viral video! There is nothing cooler than seeing a concept in your head blossom into a project that people like. More people seemed to share my enthusiasm and sense of humor because the next thing I knew, the video went viral. With over 3 million views, it was shared over Facebook and Twitter. I had friends and family messaging me to tell me that there was a music video that was circling the internet and the girl in it looked just like me!

I got requests from viewers for me to upload more content, and my channel traffic began to grow. The positive feedback inspired me to do more and gave me the confidence to express myself even more than I already had. I realized that I could use my *YouTube* platform not only as a way to express myself but also as a way to be discovered and prove the naysayers wrong. It worked for people like Soulja Boy, Jimmy Fallon, Kate Upton, and Justin Bieber. Why couldn't it work for me? I got to continue to do what I loved and still hold onto the potential of breaking into the entertainment industry.

For me, *YouTube* became a community of people who made it safe to talk about my day, my dislikes, and my trials: whatever was on my mind. I really loved sharing my creativity with like-minded people. I learned to grow a thicker skin from the negativity, and I realized that my subscribers became my online family. I thought to myself that most families are identified by their last name. I wanted to give my group of subscribers a name they could identify with, something that made them belong to me and me to them. I began starting my vids with **"What's up Crazies?"** I loved this opening line. 'Crazy' is how people identified me and my antics, and I thought it was the perfect description for me and my merry band of subscribers.

I started to branch out on other social media. I interacted with my fans on Twitter, talking about different events in pop culture, problems they were having, or just general discussions. The online world fascinated me. It evolved from the days when snail mail was the only means of communication to the instant gratification of the Twitterverse at your fingertips. I could bounce ideas off of my audience, follow trending topics to keep up to date on current events, or use it as an online journal for my thoughts and feelings. Fans started to seek me out for my opinions or thoughts on both **YouTube** and Twitter, so I started to gear my channel towards my views on different topics that came up both in my everyday life and based on what people asked me. My channel was a great place to hear other people's ideas and opinions and to see how they compared to mine.

Even though I found YouTube I had to find a means of making money. It was so hard to go from having a job and money to having $0.00 in your bank account. So I was looking for jobs in my area. I got a job at a restaurant shortly after. I worked there for a week, but I left because I kept getting people's orders wrong. I remember one time I tried to open a bottle of wine and spilled wine all over myself and the customer; I was so embarrassed. Things were getting serious with my boyfriend and me, or at least I thought so. He helped me shoot a few of my videos. He shot and edited my **"Hold Yuh"** parody that went "viral" on YouTube. His Mom was buying a bigger place. She wanted me to move in with them and help them pay rent. I was down! Two weeks later, my boyfriend and I split up after I asked him for a key. I guess he wasn't ready for the huge commitment. After the breakup, I moved in with my grandma because I didn't want to play Cinderella at Dad's house.

Shortly after, I got a new job at a retail department store called The Bay. Just like in any other job, I remembered having a rough day. So I came home and ranted on video about my pet peeves about working in retail. I mean really? Do customers leave clothes all over the floor at home or work? Why is it acceptable at my job? I get that it is supposed to be a customer service-driven environment, but I am still a human being. I got lots of feedback from subscribers with supportive responses and their own nightmarish experiences in customer service. I always wondered, though, if so many people know it is a problem, then why doesn't it ever improve? One customer asked me if she could get a top for a dollar because it's been on the sales rack for over six months. Really, lady? For a buck? Does this look like a garage sale to you? We do not bargain in department stores. I can rant all day and night about my nightmarish experiences working in retail!

My boss was the hardest lady to deal with. She would hide behind clothing racks, making sure we did our job, and then pop out to tell us a million and one things that we were not doing correctly. Like, she would be so angry that the hangers were not spaced out evenly. Whenever she would come into our section, we would all run pretending to do things like space hangers even though they were spaced out perfectly -- I couldn't stand her! I dreaded my job. I rolled out of bed every morning to go to a job that I couldn't stand, I wasn't happy, I was on the verge of depression. Creating content kept me hopeful that I would be able to live my dream one day.

Take Risks Or Die Hesitating

I still remember the day I gave my notice at The Bay. I went in on a day I wasn't scheduled to talk to my manager. I remember being so nervous because we had a very contentious working relationship. Belatedly, I realized that I was just nervous about the unknown. At the time I was considering YouTubing full time, but it wasn't considered a job at the time, as it was still very taboo. Reality TV and vlogging was still considered abstract - a frivolous pastime only afforded to celebrities or people who were independently wealthy.

So what gave me the courage to quit? While I was working in the retail department full-time, I would make **YouTube** videos in my spare time. Quickly, it became my passion. I looked at **YouTube** as my part-time job. I pictured myself becoming a huge entertainer, getting a reality show about my relationships with my crazy family and friends. I always had something bizarre going on in my life, which I thought would make a spectacular show. The things that were going on in my life were so fun and crazy that I just knew viewers would find this very entertaining. I got called crazy all the time by my viewers, so I started calling my viewers 'crazies' and they loved it!

In my earlier video recordings, I created an imaginary boyfriend named "Rayshawn." I would always blame things that were just outlandish on this imaginary boyfriend, and viewers found it hilarious. They were always wondering if Rayshawn existed (I recorded a video back in 2013 called: 'Looking for my Baby Daddy Rayshawn'). My cousin, Myles, recorded the entire thing, and we drove all around Toronto asking random people on the streets if they saw my baby daddy. I remember driving through the drive-thru at Mc Donald's and asking if they saw Rayshawn. I went to the food court of a mall, and I shouted "has anyone seen my baby daddy?" I clearly do not have any shame at all. Having this imaginary character was good material that helped amplify my content, and I ran with it consistently.

Now, this was way before Rapper Yo Gotti came out with the song **"Sliding in the DMs."** But it was a typical social media practice already happening on Facebook. I always kept on top of my Facebook messages so that I didn't miss any branding deals or opportunities. There were always thirsty, random guys trying to holler at me. Tadaa! A suitable candidate to be my real Rayshawn had slid his way into my inbox through a message on Facebook with his non-smiling Facebook profile photo accompanied by a smooth message about doing "business" together. To me, this was another one of those **"let's just be friends"** type of schemes. Nevertheless, I thought he was cute, and his collaboration idea had merit. We met up and shot the video for his idea, and it did surprisingly well. I've always been a sucker for a guy who knows what they want and is ambitious with it. "Rayshawn" will always tell you he was only approaching me on strictly business, but considering that we started dating shortly after, and we are now married, I am not sure if I believe him.

"Rayshawn" was good material for my videos. I could talk about our arguments, my frustrations and all the good things "Rayshawn" did for me. Looking back now, it's funny how many times I called "Rayshawn" my baby daddy; I was foreshadowing my own life without even knowing. Sometimes I wonder if, subconsciously, I always knew we would end up married and raising a beautiful family. There is something special about having someone in your life who supports all your hopes and dreams and holds you down no matter what you desire.

Slowly, **YouTube** was starting to become more and more my priority. Was it time to make the jump to full-time YouTuber? "Rayshawn"—who I eventually revealed was actually named Adam—and I started living together. What happened if **YouTube** didn't work out? Or if I had low viewership one month? Sometimes you have to take risks to do what you love, right? Yes, I had the potential to fail, but I was surrounded by people I loved who supported me.

"Rayshawn" always taught me that fear is a good indicator and that you should pursue your dreams. He told me that if I'm not happy at my job, then I need to quit. "Rayshawn" saw that I wasn't happy at my job and that I wanted to follow my dreams, and he was my number one supporter. If it weren't for him, I would probably still be at The Bay contemplating if I should leave or not. The uncertainty may be real, but being hopeful is key. Failure only happens when you stop trying. Once I handed in my resignation, the relief that came over me was massive. My manager wasn't very supportive of me handing in my resignation, and she told me that I wasn't going to succeed. But with the support of some of the people in my life, I became a full-time **YouTuber**.

When you are motivated and determined to succeed in something, fear just drives you to try harder. I didn't really have personal examples of people to aspire to be when I started out on **YouTube**. There was no REAL success just yet because the majority of the creators were just starting to build solid traction on the **YouTube** platform. So I created my niche and became my own role model. After I quit my job, I focused on recording entertaining content for people to enjoy. I had so much more time to focus on my craft and become better every video I shot. One of the greatest parts of being my own boss was not having to wake up every morning to take the bus and train to slave away at a job I hated. Instead, I woke up every day thanking God for my life.

The best advice I could give someone is to lean on those that support you. But at the end of the day, you have to look out for yourself. Throughout my journey, there have been people who didn't understand why I produced the content that appeared on my channel. I was ridiculed and told to go "get a real job". I would never let anyone tell me what my dreams should be. I embraced the journey that I chose, which helped to diminish my fear of the destination.

> She told me that I wasn't going to succeed. But with the support of some of the people in my life, I became a full-time YouTuber.

Being someone who lived paycheck to paycheck, I felt like my dream was simple: to live a comfortable life doing what I loved. My happiness came partly from making people feel good about themselves and making them smile. Even in the early days of my career, it inspired me to know that I was becoming someone who inspired others. I started dreaming even bigger: about maybe writing a book, having my own show, launching my own makeup line. The possibilities were endless. There is something about living your dreams that makes you realize that you can conquer anything you set your mind to do. I took the first step instead of hesitating.

Once I started YouTube full-time, I began to meet other video creators who were on a similar path as me, and I was more than willing to collaborate and bounce ideas around. It was like quitting my old job helped free the cobwebs over my eyes. I would always think of new ideas. My creativity was endless. Even with self-imposed deadlines, I never felt the pressure. When you love what you do, it should feel 'right,' and it did for me.

Collaborating with other YouTubers was one of my favorite parts of starting out. Having people to network and grow with gave me a sense of family. In late 2013, I begged Adam to leave his job to manage my brand. I wanted him to work on the business side of things full-time. I started to get a lot of emails from brands that wanted to work with me. It was overwhelming for me, and I would be so stressed out. I remember just staring

> 50 Cent says:
> "Get rich or
> die trying."
>
> LaToya says:
> "Take risks or
> die hesitating."

at emails from companies and not knowing how to respond. I didn't know how to write emails; I didn't know what amounts to ask for; all I knew how to do was create content. Adam was always a great business person, so I trusted him to handle the business side of things.

Adam was working behind the scenes. He worked on getting brand deals. He worked on implementing SEO best practices, branding, and website development. At times he helped write videos ideas. He played—and still plays—a big role in my career. Things were going great. They were so great that I wanted to move to LA in January 2014. I made the decision to move to LA to network and collaborate with other creators. Looking back, I realize that I did not give Adam the option to say no. He knew he had to come for our relationship to work out, and I was just so determined to make it big.

In January of 2014, Adam and I decided to move to Los Angeles. Tons of up-and-coming YouTubers were based out of there, and some of the most popular names resided here. I got to meet people I had previously only video chatted with online (Shout out to Missy Lynn, ULoveMegz, YoMuslceBoi, MysticGotJokes, and many more). It was truly the first time I was ever 100% happy with my job. I grew so much as a video creator on YouTube. I was finally doing something I loved.

One of my goals in LA was to get in shape. I lived in Hollywood, and the street I used to live on led to Runyon Canyon. Every time I would step foot out of my condo, I would see the best bodies in Hollywood. Most people had toned bodies, and it was incredibly motivating. I ate super healthy. Adam was a personal trainer, so he trained me five times a week. I remember being always drained. But no matter how healthy I ate, no matter how much I worked out, no matter how many naps I took, I was ALWAYS exhausted. One day, my girl, Maya, flew in from New York. She stayed with us for a week. She inquired about my working out, and said she didn't notice a change in my body. I was kind of upset about that because I noticed a slight difference. I remember that night I was trying to take a fitness selfie in the mirror for Instagram and using all my might to suck in my belly.

Adam was in Toronto handling some business at this time. Maya suggested that we go to CVS Pharmacy and pick up a pregnancy test. She wanted to video record the entire experience! I did not believe I was pregnant. Despite being tired, I just thought it was because I had changed up my diet and started this new workout lifestyle. Maya and I picked up a pregnancy test, and we went back to my condo. I peed on the stick and gave it right to Maya. 15 seconds went by, and Maya told me that I'm not pregnant. I then said: THANK GOD! But a few seconds later, Maya looked closer, gasped for air, and told me to take another one. I kept asking Maya if I was pregnant because I still didn't want to look at the test. She wasn't answering me. I started cursing at her as she took her sweet time trying to figure out if what she was seeing was REAL. This test took me through an emotional rollercoaster! A few moments after, the test was positive!

Little did Adam and I know that we were on the verge of the biggest responsibility adventure of our lives. A family was going to come a lot sooner than we thought.

Scared Shitless

Have you ever had the desire to take a leap of faith? Wanted something so bad, but you were afraid of what people would think? Afraid that you would fail? That is how I felt before I decided to try YouTube full-time. I knew I would be misunderstood and judged by some people who wouldn't consider it a "real" job. But sometimes to see what God has in store for you, it seems apparent that you have to take a leap of faith. I see where I am today with my two beautiful children and my loving, supportive husband. I am so thankful that I found it within me to be courageous enough to take that leap of faith.

I was already programmed to believe that life was about survival. I saw my mom do her best to get by on a daily basis. Growing up, I remember our hot water getting cut off because Mom couldn't afford to pay the bill. Sometimes she would have to boil water for us over the stove so we could take our morning showers. I knew I could have lived an easier life living with my dad's side of the family, but I felt the need to stick by Mom's side through the hard times. Whatever she was going through in life, I wanted to be there for her. A lot of people think that because my dad was a professional baseball player that I must have lived a plush lifestyle. Yes, I had cool things, but I honestly felt bad a lot of the time because my brothers and sister didn't have those things. I remember my sister, Tani, always saying: **"LaToya is Mom's favorite"** because I got a lot of clothes and things. A lot of the time, I would allow my sister to wear jeans from my DKNY jean collection (I had over ten pairs). I felt bad because I had so much stuff, so I would share with my sister. I remember when we would get in fights because she would come home with my jeans dirty. She had this habit of wiping her food on her pants, and she would always bring my jeans back with stains.

As I've gotten older, it's become apparent to me why I always had jobs that I dreaded. It's because that seemed like the way of survival. Quickly, I began to adopt a different mindset. I started reading more and understanding how successful people think and do. Successful people find ways to change things they do not like. There is no sense in being miserable with any part of your life. It only adds unnecessary stress. Adam helped me realize that I needed to make that first choice to invest in myself. Slowly, I began to believe that the person that values me the most was me, and I needed to put myself first.

Seeing my dad's success motivated me to work hard to achieve my dreams. Growing up, I wanted to be just like my dad. I looked up to him, and he was successful. I wanted to live my passion and get paid for it. I wanted to be famous and drive a Range Rover just like Dad. I remember, when Dad played baseball in Japan. After his baseball games, fans would chase my dad's car and ask for pictures and autographs. I remember this Japanese boy named Makoto would always run up to the car and give me Japanese grape bubble gum. Makoto and I became friends, and he would go to my dad's practices with me. He would come over and hang out. Yes, I had a crush on him, but we didn't speak the same language. I remember purchasing a Japanese/English

> I took that leap of faith and pumped out content.

book and that's how we would communicate. My cousins, Ana and Tenesha, would come out to Japan to keep me company. My stepmom got Ana and I a Japanese tutor so we could learn how to speak the language (more like be able to understand my crush Makoto).

YouTube was the perfect platform for me to create videos and become one step closer to being just like my dad. Starting a new venture is always a scary risk. Back then, I cared about what people thought about me. Family members would tell me that I was wasting my time, ask me why was I embarrassing myself, tell me that I'm making a fool out of myself and that I would regret it when I got older...the list goes on. Talk about dream killers! I took that leap of faith and pumped out content. When I first started to create videos, I was so nervous. I was always nervous when storyboarding ideas, wondering how people were going to react and if it was fresh and original enough. Was I still being authentic? Was this actually how I felt about the situation? Was it a step forward or a step back? All these questions had no answers, so I decided to put myself out there. YouTube was the space I could be 100 percent my crazy and wacky self. Eventually, I became comfortable acting like the person I wanted to be that I was the same person off-camera as well. I started pumping out content, and a lot of the feedback was great. A lot of people thought my videos were hilarious.

I was struggling with treading the line between being myself and keeping people happy. All it takes is one time for the tide to turn and everyone to hate me. At the beginning, that was my ultimate fear: that people wouldn't care what I had to say. Worse that they would hate me and everything I stood for. I learned to trust in my struggle and that nothing that was worth anything ever came quickly. Starting a new venture is always a scary risk. I have to give credit to all my fellow Vloggers out there; I now realize how hard it is. Developing original content that pleases viewers but also stays true to yourself is a delicate line to tread. So many times I thought about quitting and going to work in the corporate world. Many of my friends were in university, or starting out in their new careers, and then had jobs that were 9-5 on Monday through Friday. And while those jobs all came with their own set of difficulties, they seemed to make my friends a lot less stressed than I was.

It's funny how people's lives always look a lot easier from the outside. It's human nature to want to take the path of least resistance. In the early days, I yearned for the routine and regularity even though I knew that I wasn't cut out for a desk job. In a corporate job, the buck didn't stop with me. So as long as I did what I was told, I would get a paycheck every two weeks. As a YouTuber, my financial earnings were dependent on my production. I was the boss of myself. Therefore, I had to hold myself accountable. And while that may have been a lot of responsibility, I was doing what I loved. And since when has a challenge been a bad thing?

People always ask me how I deal with haters and the negative comments online. When I was first starting out, these keyboard warriors intimidated me big time. The fact that people who didn't even know me had such hatred for me was just mind boggling. I've had arguments with people in real life, but I have never had anyone actively hate me for just existing. The online sphere is full of keyboard warriors whose sole goal in life is to make you stop pushing for what you want. People say negative things about me, about my family, and my friends. Basically they are faceless online bullies. I do not condone this type of activity, and I now have a team to moderate it as much as possible on my channels. I have developed a thick skin, but I do not think my children or friends or family should be subjected to this negativity just for being associated with my name.

> *I was the boss of myself. Therefore, I had to hold myself accountable.*

At first, I used to take the comments personally, but then I realized that these people don't actually know me. Keyboard warriors take the small snippets of your life that you choose to share and assume that they know your entire life. I try and make sure I show as much of my life as I can, but I do like to keep a lot of things private. Regardless, the judgment and the assumption that you know everything about me because of what you see is wrong. The profanity, the telling me I am a bad person, and various other things I cannot write here unless I want my book to end up in the "Adult" section, is just unnecessary. If people do not like me or what I have to say, then they have the option to just turn off their screen.

I will never understand the drive of these people to go and regularly watch my videos and social media and then attack me online. These are always the people with private pages or no picture in their profile, and they are usually projecting their own insecurities onto whomever they are attacking. These people even create forums and communities to defame my character and try to "take me down," I will never understand why people go out of their way to bring others down. I admit that I am sometimes controversial or say outrageous things. But I just want to get my ideas and thoughts out there. I do not believe I deserve to be attacked for those views, but I take the good and the bad, and that's the way the web goes today. Trolling my page or creating content just to bring me down just shows the person's character.

> I admit that I am sometimes contro-versial or say out-rageous things. But I just want to get my ideas and thoughts out there.

I wish I could tell myself this when I first started out. A few times, some of the comments really upset me to the point of crying and thinking of quitting. But one day I realized that I am doing what I love, and people will be envious, bitter and petty about my success. I cannot worry myself about what people think. For every negative person, I have 1000 Huntys and Huncles who love me for who I am.

There is no greater feeling than waking up every morning and knowing you are in charge of your own destiny. It makes a stronger person knowing that you alone need to navigate through any hurdles in your life. It ensures you wake up every morning with a passion for life, wanting to tackle your everyday challenges and become a better person.

Looking back now, I realize that part of that feeling of insecurity was because I wasn't entirely comfortable with myself. I go after what I want without any apologies, and I encourage people to do the same. I find it interesting that I was struggling so much just to put my ideas out there for people to judge; now I love to do it. Don't forget, trust in your struggle, and never leave home without the three Fs: Family, Friends, and Fans!

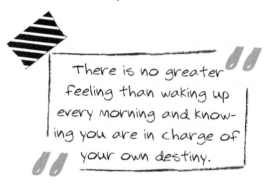

There is no greater feeling than waking up every morning and knowing you are in charge of your own destiny.

One of my funniest high school memories was in the old days of Black Planet, Myspace, and MSN. My bestie, Ayanna, and I decided to create our own page on Black Planet; we called ourselves *"De Plastix"* after the greatest movie of all time, Mean Girls. We used to be told how much we looked alike and that we could pass for sisters. Ayanna is the sister of my heart. Even though she sometimes seems shy, she is just as loony as I am sometimes. We rolled with the sister idea and had our photo shoot. We took this new sisterly bond way too seriously, and in hindsight, the page was an insane thing to do. We didn't do it for attention, though, we were just having fun and being silly. I try and base my YouTube life around that experience.

People may not understand it, and they may hate or reject the idea, but as long as my friends, family and I are having fun, that is what matters the most.

My friends and family started to support my dreams, and they started appearing in some of my videos too. I love that my friends and family are all different, but all embrace my over-the-top, *"Trini to di bone"* personality. It was great that they could just be themselves and let go even with a camera in the room. My cousin, Myles, and I started to come up with funny challenges and skits to do at my grandma's house. She used to get so mad at us, yelling at how "stchupid" we were. The best video I think was the cinnamon challenge when Myles and I ended up dry heaving over my grandmother's sink. We told her that we were dying while coughing out the cinnamon into the sink, and she told us to call 911!

It's crazy how much we forget the things that are important to us as a child and the life lessons we learned. I had so many experiences where I was shown that I should just be myself, but even in my late teens, I was trying to do things because my friends were doing them and not because they truly made me happy. All my friends going to school and getting an education. Here I am, clueless on what to major in. Why was this happening to me? What was I doing so wrong? I had to wake up, listen to my voice, and figure out what made me happy. What made me happy was entertaining people. I've always had a passion for making people laugh, I've always said that I wanted to get paid to be me, and I would always laugh about it with my friends.

My mom was a believer in me. Mom is my #1 fan. I remember telling my mom that I wanted to get paid to live my life, and Mom always said: *"LaToya, you were born a star, and you can be anything you want to be."* That year I said: *"You know what, I'm going to get paid to be myself."* I'm going to build my brand." I created profiles across all social media. I went to acting auditions, modeling auditions, entered contests to become a Video Jockey, and submitted applications to be on different reality shows. I just put myself out there. I hosted weekly live shows on **BlogTV**. I remember I used to trend every time I would have a show, and it was so fulfilling to me to have so many people who enjoyed my work. They inspired me to keep on going. I then created a YouTube channel in 2009, and I continued creating content for people to enjoy. I'm just so grateful that I listened to my heart and followed through with my dreams. I made those dreams a reality. Sometimes, it takes being lost to find yourself.

Viewers Need To Understand

Being comfortable in your own skin is something that **YouTube** has taught me. Fans can immediately tell when someone is authentic or fake for the camera. I quickly learned that being myself was in everyone's best interest since it requires less energy and less thinking. When I am myself, I can have genuine connections with my fans, which is important to me. I've been on camera in full glam, no glam, sick, well, and everything in between. Being accepted no matter what is such a blessing. When I was younger, I was always trying to fit in. *"Why are you trying so hard to fit in, when you were born to stand out"* is one of my favorite movie quotes (and one of the most relevant to my life). I had such a hard time when I was trying to be something I was not. Now that I just live in my truth, I am so much happier. No more worrying if people would ever like who I was underneath all the layers. I put myself out there every time a camera is on.

As a vlogger, I get to live my life to the fullest. Being your own boss and getting to share your creativity with the world is one of the coolest aspects of living the online life. I get to travel the world to meet my supporters and network with amazing

> Being your own boss and getting to share your creativity with the world is one of the coolest aspects of living the online life.

people. I also get to work with some of the best brands in the world like **TOYOTA, SPRITE, PAMPERS, AUDIBLE** and so many more. Moreover, an outcome I didn't expect was how involved my family and friends got in my new venture. My Auntie Jillian, my brother-in-law Aaron, my best friend Ayanna and her husband Kevin, my bestie Rochelle, and bestie Chanelle have all started successful YouTube channels. People always ask how I feel about their successes, and the truth is that I love it!

My family bonds have grown stronger, and I've learned to distinguish my true friends from the not so real. Having supportive family and friends is important to me. I learned very quickly who was just around for the cameras and who was sincerely supportive of my dreams. In a way, I think of my vlogging as a family business. If I need a sick day, or help with some creative ideas or concepts, I have my team there for me. It means there is never a dull moment in the Ali house. Sometimes I wonder if my house is a home or a hotel/office space. I love all my friends and family, but shoot! Can a girl be able to take off her wig in peace?!

Another aspect of this online life that I am grateful for on this journey is my fans. My Huntys and Huncles have supported me through my struggles and helped shape me to be who I am today. To be in the **YouTube-sphere**, you need to have a very thick skin. From when I became a full-time YouTube personality, the negative slander being posted on my page was certainly overwhelming. People can sometimes be very quick to hate those who they do not understand. I had people trying to dig up mistakes from my past and people blatantly lie about me.

Sometimes people forget that behind the **YouTube** personality is a real person with genuine feelings and emotions. But, conversely, seeing all the lives I impact through my daily antics of being myself or my video recording skits makes me want to persevere. I heard once that haters are just fans in denial. That statement has some truth in it. People who claim to hate me online are the first people who are on my social media pages watching the videos and disliking them. Those are the people I hope will get it together, find the happiness they are looking for and begin to live a life of positivity to uplift others instead of trying to bring them down. Unfortunately, there is another downside to the online world: with only a few clicks, you are very accessible. Online users tend to forget that behind the **YouTube** personality is a person with real feelings. I love interacting with my fans when I meet them in everyday life, but there are boundaries and I wish that people would respect that. The problem is that there is no fan etiquette manual when dealing with online influencers because this is a relatively new world.

Being a mother is one of the most rewarding parts of my life. I am like a mama bear with my two cubs. No one messes with them. I remember I was driving my kids to the walk-in clinic and a lady was tailing me. I tried to dodge her and continue with my day. As soon as I parked, the woman jumped out of her car and approached me. I took pictures with her and spoke to her for a little bit. Looking back, I remember how uncomfortable the interaction made me feel. This fan followed me in my car around my neighborhood. I felt stalked. My kids weren't feeling well that day. My intention is never to offend my fans. So it's hard to figure out when it's ok to say no. I just wish people thought about how they would feel if they experienced some of the things done to me. I'm a real person just like them. Put yourself in my shoes. Having to be "on" all the time can be exhausting.

> Online users tend to forget that behind the YouTube personality is a person with real feelings. I love interacting with my fans when I meet them in everyday life, but there are boundaries...

I remember another time when I answered my front door and a viewer was standing on my doorstep. She quickly said she was a subscriber that she would normally not do this, that it's out of her character, but she's a really big fan. I looked at Adam. Before I could open my mouth and say anything, Adam stopped me. We allowed her to continue talking about how much she loves our videos and how her kids watched our videos. She asked how Samia was and asked if she could say hi and so forth. When we wrapped up our conversation, I was livid. I felt violated. I couldn't believe someone would knock on the door of someone they didn't know.

It's not authentic for me to be happy and cheery all the time. Real people feel all different types of emotions. I am a mother first and foremost. And that is one thing I wish that people would realize. I think one of the differences between being a **YouTube** personality and an actress is how people see your life. Actors and Actresses play characters on TV, and their private lives stay separate, for the most part, unless it is plastered over tabloids or entertainment news. Some celebrities choose to live outside the public eye to maintain some anonymity. This privacy gives them mystery and makes them seem less accessible. When your screen life is based on your real life, people assume that they have the right to unlimited access to all aspects of your life. There is no privacy because you aren't playing anyone but yourself. Adam, Samia, Zayn and I love sharing our lives with the world, but we also need private time as a family.

Your fans can make or break you. Sometimes I would see someone write hateful things on my page, but before I could even find myself pressed about it, they would already be shut down by one of my faithful fans. To feel that kind of love and support from people I have never met just gave me a greater sense of purpose and drive. Because of this, I started to have meet and greets. I wanted to meet all of the amazing people that wanted to support me on my journey.

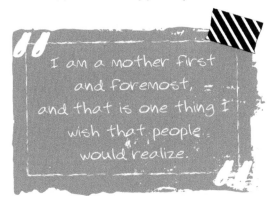

I am a mother first and foremost, and that is one thing I wish that people would realize.

#pitbull #minnesota

#hunty #vlogging

#Living_the_Dream

#Onstage

I remember a fan in the London, England, where nearly 1000 people came to see me, but I remember this one specific fan because she touched my life. I was chatting with some fans, and suddenly someone approached me with multiple cuts on her arm. I've never encountered someone who was a cutter. I was immediately nervous. I only knew about mental illness in theory, and I wasn't sure what to expect. I was overwhelmed when she got emotional and told me how my story touched her life. I was stunned, and I offered my sincere empathy and encouraged her to stop cutting and love herself. I just couldn't imagine that my story had touched another person so deeply. I was humbled.

Anytime I am frustrated with anything related to **YouTube**, I reflect on that hunty. It feels good to know that I can make a difference in the world even if I am not actively trying to do so. I got in this business for fun, but I continue it because of supporters like her that make me feel like I can do anything and help anyone just by being myself. So to any fan that has ever felt like I slighted them, or didn't have enough time for them, I apologize. I appreciate every single one of you, and you all touch my life just as much as I hope I may have touched yours.

I have always suffered from wanderlust. Vlogging has sent me all over the continental U.S., to Dubai, London, the Bahamas, Barbados, etc. I've met so many fans around the world, networked with amazing YouTube personalities, and gotten to experience different cultures. Getting to give that gift of travel to myself and my family is a dream come true at such a young age.

Interviewing celebrities has been rewarding, and I look forward to meeting many more. Listening to their insight on how they deal with being in the public eye is motivating. The fact that I am considered a peer with people that I idolized growing up is something I will never grasp. I got to attend a Pitbull concert in Minnesota and interview him on behalf of Cricket Wireless. Pitbull was down to earth and very motivational. I remember he knew my family was Trinidadian just by looking at me. I'm noticing more than ever that high-caliber celebrities and iconic figures have positive rituals and are great at making people feel comfortable. That is a skillset I still need to work on, as I have been told I can be somewhat unapproachable. I want to give off positive energy at all times. YouTube Celebrity Tyler Oakley and I got flown to New Orleans for the Pepsi Super Bowl after party for Beyoncé. I also got to host a red carpet at the American Music Awards for Vibe magazine. I remember being star-struck as stars walked down the carpet. I walked the same path as **J. Cole, Tyga, Chris Brown, 50 Cent** and many more!

Happiness is not a trophy that you receive and shelve. It is an energy that you continuously pursue and radiate on others. I pray to always pursue happiness and always be able to share my joy with the world.

"
New York is the city
that never sleeps,
the place where I
got engaged to the
love of my life, and
the place where I
met many Youtubers.
"

Seeing The World

When I was in high school, I would have never believed that I would grow up to be a familiar online personality, married, and mom of two. YouTube has opened up so many opportunities for me and allowed me to connect with people from various places around the world. I've been blessed to attract fans from the cities of Los Angeles, Miami, London, Australia, Trinidad, and Dubai. And those are just a few places where I have a fanbase! I'm international, baby!

My life, which happens to be my brand, has attracted many viewers around the world. It's beyond anything I could have imagined, and the thought that I am just touching the surface can be a scary. I have two YouTube channels, and one of them has over a million subscribers. I also have an online apparel store. Now, I have a book! I am currently in beta phases for many new business ventures that I look forward to launching soon.

Traveling all over the world is a blessing in itself, but being able to do it with my family is even better. Showing my children the world and letting them learn about different

cultures is precious to me. One notable and exotic location I got to visit was Dubai, UAE. The architecture there is insane. All the buildings were beautiful. Pictures just don't do Dubai justice. My family and I loved the resort hotel we stayed in, and even though it was hot and I sweated out of my perm, it was no doubt a memorable period. I ate so much food while I was there. I remember when some beautiful fans took my family out for dinner at a very elegant restaurant that was adjacent to the Burj Khalifa tower. It was an amazing view that I could never forget.

You know I had to make a stop at the largest mall in the world: Dubai Mall. They had every store you could think of, and I bought so much stuff. I wouldn't mind living in Dubai part-time during the year. I could even survive the heat for all that beauty. The scenery, the people, the animals—it's such a beautiful city. I got to see camels for the first time, and they are massive. Camels just sit on the beach all day. All I could think was: aren't they hot? I almost fell off the camel, though, from like 10 feet high. I figured I was going to plummet to my death! Adam was just laughing at me the whole time and shaking his head. The way they just drop down at the end of the ride, Lord have mercy!

I got a few requests to host a meet and greet in Dubai. I thought maybe a handful of people would show up, since I wasn't too sure I had a following in the United Arab Emirates. Knowing how much I enjoy connecting with my loyal supporters, I knew I had to have a meet and greet here. I was shocked when almost 100 people showed up. I was shocked that I was able to attract people to come out, especially in the Middle East. It hit me that I had viewers all over the world. Two girls from my meet and greet wanted to show us around Dubai's hotspots. We walked over to this restaurant nearby, and there were these massive palm trees with water everywhere. It was incredible. They treated us to dinner, which was so sweet, and we got to see how locals live and eat there. We also got to see this cool water fountain show that was choreographed to music with the Burj Khalifa in the background. Everyone I met in Dubai was kind, respectful and friendly. Best birthday gift ever!

I've also had the opportunity to visit all different states in the U.S. When we visited L.A., we got to see all the famous sites with our L.A.-based YouTubers, Nikki and John. They took us to a private ranch where we got to meet a movie Giraffe. I missed being in L.A. For the few months I lived there before I had Samia, it was awesome. Plus, the food is usually healthy. My friend Niena introduced Adam and me to this fabulous restaurant called Bosonova, which serves Brazilian food. The wait time is always at least 2 hours, but it's totally worth it. Their chicken skewers and seasoned shrimp are the food of the gods! Before Niena introduced us to the Bosonova restaurant, I remember craving

Chipotle every day. I made Adam visit that restaurant so many times that we eventually got sick of it. In hindsight, I realize that it was Samia that was demanding Mexican food in the womb (this was before I knew I was pregnant).

Miami was another fantastic destination. The house we stayed in was spacious. It had multiple kitchens and a waterfall pool in the backyard. I usually just travel with my family, but this time we brought my friends De'Laila, Kyle, Ayanna and Kevin straight after their engagement. I loved being able to spend some quality time with my friend after her great news. Adam suggested we give them the master suite so they could enjoy their time as a newly engaged couple. GabebabeTV hung out with us, and we had a meal at Dj Khaled's Restaurant. We also took a boat cruise and got to see the celebrity homes of P. Diddy and Oprah. It's always inspiring to see how people can turn ideas into a plush life.

My meet and greet in Miami was successful! I remember getting out of the car in the Wynwood Walls Art District and hearing people start screaming my name. All these beautiful Miami people just touched my heart. There was this one little girl that was crying with excitement to meet me and all my friends. It felt great to make her day. A lot of my friends hadn't done international meet and greets before, so this was cool to share with them and the fans. Miami weather, fans, food, and overall scenery was memorable, and I look forward to returning shortly.

New York is the city that never sleeps, the place where I got engaged to the love of my life, and the place where I met many YouTubers that I've become really close with. Jeana, from Prank vs. Prank, met up with me in New York to attend Beautycon. We also met up with Missy Lynn, Aaliyah Jay, Lakiastar, and PeakMill. Missy took us all under her wing and brought us to various booths at Beautycon. The amount of free products we were gifted was insane.

I left with bags full of makeup which helped me build a whole new collection to "slay." It's amazing how meeting other YouTubers can shape your career and broaden your horizons. After being out, we went back to the hotel room and decided we were going to teach Jeana how to twerk. She was actually really good. She was a bit offbeat, but her booty could "pop." I love Jeana. I remember the best piece of advice she gave me on one of our trips was not to vlog every single day because it ruins relationships. You need private time to be a family. I try to find a balance so that I keep the fans happy, but also have off-camera time to spend with my family of four.

Another YouTuber I was glad that I got to meet was Tyler Oakley. As part of a Pepsi branding deal, we flew to New Orleans; Pepsi wanted us to get fans excited for the Beyoncé halftime show at the Super Bowl. It was my first huge brand deal. I got to meet Roxy from 106& Park, watch performances by Jamie Foxx, and hit up Bourbon and Canal Street.

The house Tyler and I stayed at while we were there was gorgeous. We had a two story modern house minutes away from the Mardi Gras Strip. Everyone was outside partying, throwing beads, and having a fun time. There was this one man in an umbrella hat yelling into a microphone about us dying for being sinners and that we had to join the church. There always seem to be people like that around when others have fun... party pooper. That was one of the most 'self-learning' trips I ever took. I admire Tyler, and he gave me lots of good advice about the industry.

Prankster Mysticgotjokes in Los Angeles reached out to collaborate, and we did a video called **"What Not To Do on a First Date."** Once he started doing videos on a consistent basis, his **YouTube** channel grew substantially. It shows that consistency works when you do what you love.

(I remember giving him YouTube advice and pointers to grow his channel. Now he has millions of subscribers on both of his channels. Did I mention that he had the biggest crush on me? ha-ha)

One of my most popular viral videos is in collaboration with 4yallENT. We did a video called ***"22 Types of Students in the Classroom."*** 4yallENT are four young men who work hard on their video content. Jae, who is—safe to say—the creative lead of the group, is very talented. He does a lot of the editing, scripting, and manages the overall logistics of their business. It's always fun to work with them because it doesn't feel like work. It's fun times. They put lots of thought and work into their videos, and I respect them and their hustle so much. One thing that successful **YouTubers** manage to do on a consistent basis is thoroughly enjoy making relatable content. When you're true to your craft, you'll always meet others who are true to what they do. Eventually, you'll build meaningful relationships. This rule pretty much translates to whatever your passion in life is, not just producing videos.

London, U.K was the biggest meet and greet I have had thus far. Don't get it twisted, London shows up and shows out. It didn't even cross my mind that all those people would be there for me. The stampede to get to me was insane. It was certainly the craziest fan experience ever. I remember starting to cry, and there was so much positive energy in the air.

I remember looking at the crowd from a distance and thinking that those people weren't there for me, that a school must be nearby my meet and greet. The thought that they were all there for me was mind-boggling. We spent the beginning of the meet and greet trying to form a line, but people were too excited to follow any instructions. It was my longest meet; we were there for 5 hours. I said to myself: all these people came out to see me, and I am not leaving until everyone gets a picture.

I had a few of my friends join my family and me in London. The day before we had our meet and greet event, we did a show in London. Music artists Elhae and 11:11 performed, and MaximBady and I hosted the event. I also answered questions that fans had. I collaborated with **YouTube** Comedian **MaximBady**, and we showcased our collaboration video to the sold out venue. **MaximBady** is a local UK YouTube Star, so I played this exclusive video to the sold out venue. It was the very first show event I put on for my supporters, and I was so grateful that they were receptive to it. One thing I will say about Londoners is that their fashion sense is on point. Whenever I go out shopping, I try to find inspiration from the UK fashion scene. I also tend to shop a lot from British apparel companies.

In London, we stayed in a basement Airbnb. The scariest thing happened one day. The door locked, and we were stuck in the basement. I almost had an anxiety attack. In London, lots of windows have bars, including the ones in our place. We couldn't get out. What if there is a fire, and I have my baby in this place? I was screaming, yelling and telling Adam to call the police. I was panicking. Thank God Adam calmed my butt down, and we got out of there in one piece.

I have so many memories from all the places I got to visit and the people I have met over the years thanks to my career as a full-time vlogger on YouTube. It has challenged me and changed me. I've met some lifelong friends along the way. I look forward to continuing this journey and being able to live my authentic life that inspires people. Wherever you are, I can't wait to meet you!

When the camera is rolling, you may say something you cannot take back. Once it is out there, the internet doesn't let you forget.

Remaining Grounded

Some of my first videos I recorded on YouTube were done with my bedroom door barred shut and on the down-low, so no one knew what I was doing. My dad and stepmom could care less about the exposure I was getting. She used to force my Dad to get me to remove videos I've worked so hard on because I recorded them in their home. I understand everyone has rules—and, looking back, I should've asked for permission—but the reality is that sometimes no matter what you do there will be people who seem to become obstacles to your dream. You have to keep at it. I kept at it. I loved making videos as it allowed me to express myself, and I was going to do it by any means necessary. At least then I would know I had tried all avenues before moving on to something else.

One of the people that helped me to keep going in my adolescence was my mother. No matter how big my dreams, she always made me believe I could do them. One of the things I wanted to do was sing and dance. I would sing in the shower, on the toilet, and along with the radio. In my head, I was going to be the next Mariah Carey. If this was my dream, then she was going to ride it with me no matter what. So Mom got me a vocal coach.

> At least then I would know I had tried all avenues before moving on to something else.

My first lesson was mortifying. I remember my vocal instructor sitting at her piano, and she told me to sing the notes as she played them on her piano: **"DO RAY MI FA SOL LA TI DO."** She had the biggest smirk on her face when I sang the notes. Then when I hit DO—the highest note—my Instructor busted out laughing! She was crying laughing. She told me that I needed a lot of work. Thank God I had a sense of humor. I laughed it off and continued my lessons. After two months of lessons, I thought I was ready to sing in front of an audience.

One day, I called my family to the living room. I told them I wanted them to hear me sing. I sang **"Heartbreaker"** by Mariah Carey. You know the part when she's hitting a range of notes near the end of the song? Well, the entire family died laughing at me. My mom, though, was so encouraging. In the early days of any career, people who support you, who always have your back, are truly blessings if you have them.

There is always one parent in the audience yelling out: **"That's my baby!"** (much to the embarrassment of everyone else around them). Don't knock that person in your life! That's unconditional love and support. As you grow and become more and more successful, it's hard to determine people's motivation. That person that rocked with you from the beginning, no matter how embarrassing, is potentially the most supportive and trustworthy person in your life.

I love my mom; she is the one who made me so comfortable in my skin. My mom, Deborah, is her own woman, and she doesn't care about anyone's opinion. No matter how outrageous or unconventional I was, she always encouraged me to be myself. Of course, you are going to make mistakes, but all you need to do is focus on mentally developing as a person. As you get older, it takes mental toughness to begin your route to whatever is it you want to accomplish. Spend your energy on evolving into a positive person, and pay no mind to people who are negative.

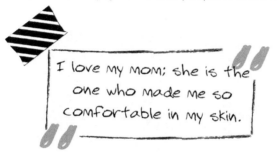

One thing that bothers me in this industry is seeing how much people are willing to give up on their pursuit. A person is only as good as their actions and their morals. It may take longer to succeed and stay authentic to you, but it will be infinitely more worth it. One thing that Adam and I always make sure to do is to be ourselves. Especially now that I have children, I am even more careful to set a good example for my son and daughter. I would never want them to think that money is more important than self. I want Samia to grow up to be a confident, motivated lady like my mom raised me.

I want Zayn to be an ambitious, self-assured man. I want my kids to know that they can do anything regardless of gender, race or any other society-perceived obstacles. And like my mom supported me, I will support their dreams whatever they may be, camera in hand and shouting "That's my baby!"

In contrast to having someone who supports you no matter what, it is important to have someone who keeps you grounded. I have been blessed to attract so many people like that in my life. I always have these huge ideas, and some would say lofty goals, but I admit that I do need to be grounded at times because being a scatter-brain is a quick, sure way to fail. It is important to know what is realistic and what isn't. It doesn't mean you cannot try; it just means that you need to keep yourself grounded and stop yourself from losing your way in ideas and not facts. Having a supportive person who deals in actualities is vital. That person in my life is my husband. Adam is my brand manager, my partner, and my filter for all things in life; he is supportive and loving in all things. However, he does keep me grounded at times like when I wanted to become a DJ.

I remember getting inspired by Paris Hilton, and all of a sudden I wanted to become a DJ. Adam was the one who pointed out the pros and cons to that idea, and showed me why it was better to hone my vlogging skills instead of dabbling. It made me feel like he was hearing me and understands my goals and needs. Adam never just shoots down an idea as stupid or frivolous. Instead, he always comes with a bigger and sometimes better idea (don't tell him I said that). To have someone shoot down your dream or idea is heartbreaking. To have them point out the flaws in your plan and say: "but hey, how about this," shows that they are just as invested in the process as you are. That person is essential in one's life.

You can attract individuals who keep you grounded and accountable when you are ambitious. How ambitious are you? Are you obsessed with what you want to achieve? If you do not think of your goal frequently throughout the day, then (I hate to break the harsh news to you) it'll be a very hard road to success. There will always be someone who has achieved the same things you want before you. The difference in that person is that they are OBSESSED in getting to their goals. Now it's never a competition against others, but there is a pie and you deserve a piece of it.

As more of my friends and family realized how seriously I was taking my new career venture, they became more supportive. At the time, I think of how frustrated I was that no one understood what I did. In hindsight, I can't blame them for how they thought about my venture.

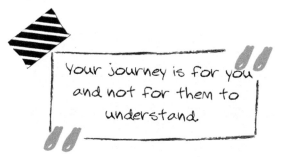

Your journey is for you and not for them to understand.

When I first started out on YouTube, it wasn't as popular as it is today. So to them, I was putting all this time and effort into something that wasn't proven (or even used as a source of income). It didn't make sense. Why would I take such a gamble with my life when I could have more guaranteed sources of revenue? Even when I first started making money, it's not like tons of money rolled in from day one. It was a painstakingly slow process. But people have to realize that there will be an equally hard struggle with every dream that is worth its weight. Oprah said that the biggest adventure you can ever take is to live the life of your dreams.

Throughout my journey, I have met and vlogged with lots of different personalities. The thing about working with people in this industry is that you aren't playing a character, so it's a bit more of an informal relationship. You don't want to associate your personal brand with someone who you don't like, which is why friendship is so important. Unfortunately, people can change and not always for the better. To remain successful and true to yourself, you sometimes have to leave people behind. If I could give anyone advice, it's that evolving is a choice. And it's a good thing. You cannot continue to associate with people who are content never to improve or want to keep you down.

> Just practice hard and stay grounded. Treat people like you want to be treated and work hard every day.

I read a book once where the main character, Gage, was trying to leave his hometown behind and improve. But every time he tried to move he felt like a crab in a box. Put a bunch of crabs in a box and they will drag down any crab trying to crawl out. The only crabs I want in my life are steamed on a plate and dipped in butter. Anytime I feel like someone is trying to hold me back, I step back and evaluate that person's part in my life. Anyone who truly loves and supports you will never try and hold you back. Even individuals who have been with you from the beginning have the potential to change. No matter what outside pressure I faced, I remembered always to remain true to myself and follow my gut instinct.

Thankfully, the majority of people in my life are unbelievably supportive of my goals. They have helped by appearing in my vlogs, sharing their lives with my fans, or just being supportive behind the scenes. For me, it's important to have support in all avenues of my life: my family, my career, and support for just me. Everyone's contribution to my life, no matter how big or small, is appreciated. I don't think I would my brand would be where it is today without my family and my friends, and I love them all so much.

Being grounded gives you the opportunity to fly.....

Samia is going to be a big sister!

My Family, Home,
And Happiness

August 20, 2011   Day Adam and LaToya met
October 12, 2014   Birth of my firstborn, Samia
March 30, 2016   Birth of my son, Zayn

Three days that completely changed my life thus far: the one when I met my husband, the one when I had my beautiful daughter, and the one when I had my handsome son. They are the three people that I am the most grateful for, and I am humbled that God blessed me with them. They are the reason I get up every day and do what I do. I want to show my children that being yourself should never be a burden or something you hide. I want them to grow up proud of who they are and trusting in their dreams. I want Adam to be proud of me as his wife and the mother of his children. As long as I remember why I am doing this, I can easily balance my online life with my real life.

Adam, Samia, and Zayn are not the only family members I am grateful for. I love all of my supportive family. My Auntie Jillian, Uncle Warren, and Cousins Myles, Milan, Ana are like my second clan. They love Samia and Zayn like their own. Sometimes I don't even need to ask for help from them. They just come over willingly and give a hand. I will be sitting at home, trying to get my day done so I can go pick up Samia from daycare, and I will get a phone call saying they want to pick Samia up from daycare and that they will bring her by later. To have such a supportive and caring family is priceless to me. With my grandparents, my mom, my dad, and all my siblings, there are so many family members that are just helpful and pleasant to my little family and me.

And while we may have our ups and down, when I need something, I know they will be there for me.

Getting pregnant with Samia forced me and Adam to make our first reality life vs. real life choice. Although we felt like being in LA was the next logical step of my career, moving back to Toronto would be a wiser decision for the benefit of my family. So we packed up our stuff and said goodbye to our life in the city of angels.

While we decided what our life as a family of three was going to look like, Adam and I stayed at my grandma and grandpa's house because we needed support with my pregnancy. Adam and I began saving and searching for our first house to buy. We went into 5th gear and started working extremely hard. I am so grateful that my grandparents supported us in that time of need when we were trying to figure it all out. Our life was taking such a crazy unexpected detour, and I am not sure what we would have done without them. I am thankful for Adam in those moments as well. I am certain it was difficult for him to live with my family. Adam is such an independent person, but he put his personal feelings aside to do what was best for his family. That, to me, is the definition of someone who sees the bigger picture and is destined to be an awesome father.

One of the craziest moments when I was pregnant with Samia was when my dad and I got into a huge argument over my baby shower. It had started between my stepmother and me. I remember wanting to have my baby shower in my dad's backyard. Dad's backyard is beautiful. He has a basketball court, pool, and a gorgeous patio. I thought it would have been perfect to have it at my dad's house. My stepmom said I couldn't have it there because they were going to do renovations. Long story short, I ended up having my baby shower at my aunt's house, and my baby shower was beautiful.

The day of my baby shower, my brother and sisters had to leave early because my stepmom was having a BBQ in her backyard. I went off on my dad, and we got into another fight. I was bawling my eyes out, telling him how his wife controls him. I went ballistic to the point where I thought I was going into pre-term labor. A lot of my followers ask where my stepmom is, and

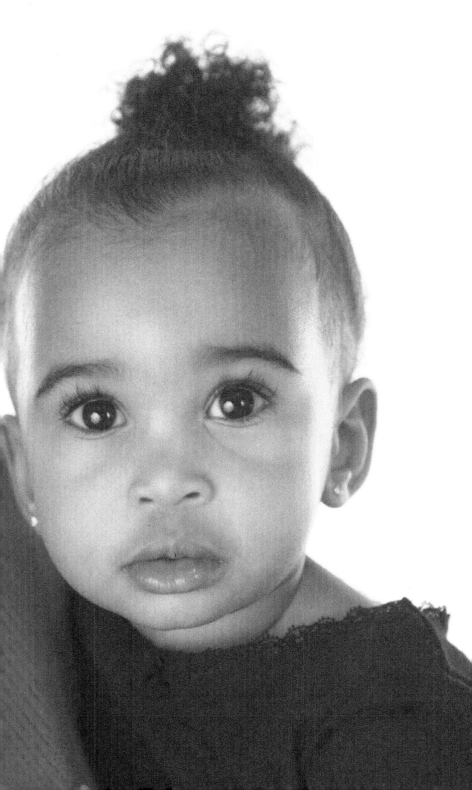

I'm telling you once and for all: we do not speak. I don't know if we will ever be on speaking terms, but I wish her well. I love her, and if I ever see her again, I will be cordial. Our personalities do not click.

With my son Zayn, I didn't have such heightened emotions (except when my brother and brother-in-law used my Range Rover for a music video and got it stuck in the mud, and I had to replace parts on my car, ha-ha). I did, however, have intense cravings. One of my cravings was drinking soda pop. It was out of control. I drank way too much of that stuff. I couldn't even drink substitutes. One of my friends even went so far as to get the caffeine-free versions and brought over a case. It sat in my fridge for other people to drink, and I went out and got the real stuff. Zayn just knew when I was trying to trick him. Even in the womb, my baby was smart!

I had the gestation period of an elephant with Zayn. My patience was wearing thin in those last few weeks. I wanted him to hurry up and get here. When I was pregnant with Samia, I did all kinds of things to induce my labor. I was so over being pregnant. I remember one day my cousin gave me a foot massage and made me eat an entire pineapple, and Samia popped out the next morning. Being pregnant with Zayn was the worst of the two. I was so over my pregnancy. So I induced Zayn as well.

> Zayn just knew when I was trying to trick him. Even in the womb, my baby was smart!

I remember one evening when I put six bags of Raspberry Leaf Tea in a cup and drank it. I also took three tablespoons of castor oil. At 3am, I was having contractions, and I had him later that morning. I had both of my babies naturally. My labor and delivery with Zayn was challenging. I learned that castor oil induces, but also intensifies your labor and delivery. And boy is that true!

I am thankful that my family supports my ever-evolving lifestyle. Without their support, it would be a lot harder to balance my reality life and my real life. Once you put your life in the public eye, not everyone is supportive. People tend to make up rumors and lies about the people you surround yourself with. You also get to see an unvarnished view of yourself, which isn't always flattering. I have had both family and friends fall out over stuff that happened while the cameras were rolling. That is one of the ugly sides of online life: things tend to take on a different connotation through the lens of a camera, especially when you have people dissecting every phrase or gesture.

Some people comment in a lighthearted way. One of my favorite fan pages is one called TheHuntyShadeRoom. It's a forum on Instagram that keeps up with the life of my family and friends and the drama that surrounds us all. People are free to comment and give their two cents on things that happen both on camera and the social media sphere. I like this page because it doesn't only concentrate on the drama. It also congratulates us on our triumphs, new babies, and engagements, sometimes even when we just happen to be wearing a particular outfit of the day that looks great and on what our generation now calls 'slaying.' Unfortunately, there are other fan pages dedicated only to bashing us all and twisting situations into something ugly and adverse. Situations like that are when your true familial bonds are tested and when you have to know the difference between online and real life.

There is nothing I hate more than when someone that is close to me assumes something and takes to social media to vent their frustrations, especially if we are close and they have my number. Adam is terrific at keeping me level-headed. As soon as someone maligns me or lies about my family or friends, I immediately want to go after them. He helps me realize that it's what they want: more attention and more views. Some people go to great lengths to create fake arguments or beef just to get in the spotlight. A real family and true friendships always keep clear communication, are always open for clarification, and are not jumping to conclusions.

As a social media influencer, I really have to be careful who I associate myself with because if I were to ever have a falling off it would most likely be in the public eye. I remember when one person I was getting close to decided that she didn't want to associate herself with me because she had a falling-out with two of my closest friends. This person decided to attack all my friends and me across all social media. She was spreading rumors and lies about me. She said things like that my vlogs are fake, that I'm not happy, that I use people, and so forth. This person even went the extra mile to bash my character across all the hate pages about me. When things went sour, she took it to social media and all hell broke loose.

People often forget that, when the camera is rolling, you may say something you cannot take back. Once it is out there, the internet doesn't let you forget, even if it was a mistake. My family and I have learned to give each other the benefit of the doubt. They say that a diamond is forged under pressure. That is a metaphor for my life. The reality sphere—and the pressure that comes with it—has shown me the bonds that are and will always be strong like diamonds and the ones that were not that strong to begin with and were meant to be temporary. There is no shame in moving on from a relationship. It's called evolution. People who are really in your corner will grow with you, and those that don't sometimes have to be left behind. It's a harsh but accurate truth.

> **My online life has helped to mold me into the woman I am today, and I wouldn't trade it for anything.**

My online life has helped to mold me into the woman I am today, and I wouldn't trade it for anything. I have been through lots of struggles, but my family and I have flourished and come out on the other side stronger than ever. I love that I get to create this life with those I love. Having my family caused me to grow up and mature faster than I believed. I am now a role model not only for others but also for my two young impressionable children. I want my kids to be proud of me. I think having my children has made my entire extended family a closer unit. I now understand a lot more about the other people in my family because of having my children. It surprised me how much my view of the world changed with just a few pushes and those two first-cries that changed my life.

I'm excited to watch my kids grow up and become their own person.

Keeping Up With LaToya

So we're here!

YouTube has been a whirlwind so far, and I feel like I'm just getting started. I still have so many ideas and tons of my life to share with my Huntys and Huncles.

Not too long ago, I had my second child, Zayn. Between him and Samia, there is never a dull moment in the Ali household. Zayn is the most demanding of my two children. It's like he knew there was already a sibling who had previously staked a claim. So he makes sure that we are aware he is there. Trust me, Zayn, Mama loves you Refusing to go to sleep without being on my chest is not the proper way to make your mark in this world!

I'm excited to watch my kids grow up and become themselves. I'm excited to see what kinds of interests they will have. Their personalities are already starting to come in. My daughter Samia is a neat freak. Anytime we have playtime or a bath, she always puts things away, whether it be her toys into the toy chest or her diaper into the toilet (YES that's happened before).

I can see little parts of both my and Adam's personality coming out in her, and it makes me so proud that we created two beautiful lives.

So what's next?

This book! I cannot believe I have a book out, and the idea that someone like you went out of your way to go chapter after chapter to see the world through my words is absolutely amazing to me. I look forward to continuing to write and put my mark on this earth!

I'm considering the beauty and makeup-up world lately. So who knows if I will start working on a makeup line soon? I'm one of those people who is always constantly mixing brands and samples to get the perfect look for me, so it would be cool to mix something to share with the world. (It blows my mind that I grew up as a tomboy and am now considering having my make-up line!) I just want something that is versatile for all different types of women.

Sometimes you don't want to do the full glam. You just want to have light coverage but still look flawless. I'm hoping to offer solutions to most, if not all, makeup necessities. I am making a lot of bold statements on what I want. I tend not to fear about putting my ideas out there to the universe. I am a firm believer in the idea that if you put it out there then you can bring it into existence.

One of the things people tell me all the time is I should have a reality show on TV. TV is cool, and if it did happen then I would explore it, but I am happy with the pace on YouTube. My family, friends and I are close to our viewers with all the Shenanigans that consistently seem to be surrounding us. Not too long ago,

I got interviewed about why people should watch my life. My answer: it's organic. We show our struggle and real drama. There are kids involved. This is real, and there are no sets or scripts. We're young media moguls trying to keep family values intact because we believe in family. We record with the goal of being **#FamilyGoals**. It's simple, but it's real!

Sure, it's nice to watch the shows where they are carrying Celine purses, switching men like fresh pairs of underwear, and turning up in the night club. I just think those shows gloss over the family side of things. Even the current shows that are on portray the biggest problems of teens today as whether to have Lil Wayne or Drake at their 16th birthday.

This is real, and there are no sets or scripts.

In the short term, something I would like to do is plan a new ritual girls trip away. I feel like I never see all my girlfriends at once. Our schedules are all so busy, and we never seem to all be in the same space at the same time. I think hanging out in some huge cabin near a spa would be fun. I want to do something out of the box: a giant road trip or flying quickly to somewhere fun and unexpected.

I'm excited for my friend Chanelle (aka Pony) to get married. Speaking of weddings, I'm also interested in exploring the idea of a wedding. Adam and I didn't have a wedding. We have never had a wedding because we had to figure out in less than seven months where we would have our newborn sleep. (After giving birth to Samia, I didn't even have time to see the house in person before we bought it. Adam found the house and called me on Facetime, and I got to see the house virtually.) I keep saying I'm going to plan my own wedding, and I never get around to it. Who knows? Maybe we might just throw a giant party for all of my friends and family to celebrate the Ali Family Unit. I want to wear a wedding dress; I've never tried one on before.

A new YouTube space just opened up in Toronto, so I'm looking forward to seeing all the exciting things they bring to the city. I hope to continue to connect with my supporters in different places around the world by hosting meet and greets. I plan to network and meet more video creators in order to, hopefully, help inspire some people as my peers and predecessors have inspired me.

I think Adam and I are done with having kids. Having two is challenging enough when you are self-employed. Maternity leave is not a thing. You have to continue to be on your grind, especially if you want to provide a bright future for all the kids you seem to be having. I have to commend my mom and all the other mothers out there who hold down jobs and raise their children. I never realized just how much hard work and dedication goes into raising a child, and Adam and I still have a long road ahead of us even if we don't have more children.

A Day in the Life
of LaToya

ne question I get regularly is what a day in my life looks like, and I thought I share with you to help you understand how we go about our day on this side of the camera. For me, I think routine is important, especially with kids. It was really hard to get both of my children on a schedule the first couple months. They would get up whenever they felt like it, and sleep whenever they wanted. Zayn and Samia could fall asleep in the middle of a conversation.

I wake up every morning around 7 am to feed Zayn, and get Samia if she is up by then, and we generally spend a few minutes in bed as some morning family time before its time to begin the day. This is one of my favorite parts of the day because it keeps me grounded and reminds me why I grind as hard as I do. It's also probably the slowest part of my day where I can just relax and soak it all in before the madness begins. Once I feed Zayn, he normally dozes for a bit and has some man time with Adam, while I go and prepare Samia breakfast while she enjoys: Max and Ruby, Little Charmers and Shimmer and Shine.

At this point I try to eat breakfast, and catch up on my messages that popped up while I slept, sometimes I wonder about my friends and family, do they ever sleep?! Throughout the night there are always people reaching out and it means a lot. There has never been a morning that I haven't woken up to a dozen messages sent at ridiculous hours; yes Cousin Tenesha I am talking to YOU!

Samia has, of course, developed her own little personality and fashion style. Thankfully we still mostly agree on what she puts on every day. But sometimes I shake my head at her choices. (Samia loves pulling open her drawer full of tutus and the first thing she says is "I want to wear pretty." She wears her princess dresses every other week to daycare ha-ha. Enter Daddy! Adam loves taking Samia to daycare on his way to the gym. I will never know what goes on in that car ride. Hopefully, my husband is teaching our baby girl how to grow up and be a

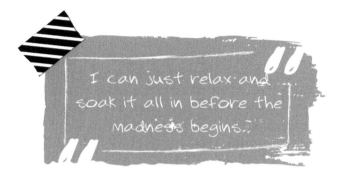

I can just relax and soak it all in before the madness begins.

strong independent woman. But I have a feeling he is lecturing her about not dating until she is at least 40!

While Adam and Samia start their day without me, I move onto my quality time with Zayn. Bath time with my son is always an interesting event. I consider it a success if I manage to keep most of the water in the tub.

At this point in the day, I am already running behind. No matter how much you try to stick to a schedule, having children is the definition of unpredictability. I normally spend my morning with my son running around the house to do some quick cleaning and wait for my production team to come over to go through my daily agenda. When it comes to my day, I like everything scheduled down to the last minute. I have a lot of things on the go on a regular basis, so I don't want to forget anyone or anything important, inadvertently. My production team is amazing and so supportive of anything I throw out there. They help me stay on track and get things done.

> I have a lot of things on the go on a regular basis, so I don't want to forget anyone or anything important, inadvertently. My production team is amazing and so supportive of anything I throw out there. They help me stay on track and get things done. As you probably know when I was building my brand I did it all on my own.

As you probably know when I was building my brand I did it all on my own. Times have changed, and I've been able to recruit a small team. Having a productive working team around is so important to keeping your brand relevant and thriving. People who are on the same page as you and want to see you win. That is who makes up my production team; I give my all to them and expect the same in return. Another important supporter that I am sure many of my followers know is my Auntie Jillian. When she can, she comes over in the morning to help me out with Zayn and anything else I need while I get dressed for the day. If she's not available, my grandmother comes and helps out during the day. It's so much fun to have her around in the mornings. It's so much fun having my family around in the mornings. Naturally, I am not a morning person, so Auntie Jillian is great at giving me a kick-start to get going and we normally bounce some of my crazy ideas around before I unleash them out to the world. She just contributes to getting those creative juices flowing. We can talk about anything in both business and life, and I love her for it.

By the time I am dressed and ready to tackle the day, my production team is off doing their assignments for the day, and Adam is home and showered from the gym working away in his office, or with the production team. My production team uses the time I am getting ready to set up my in-house studio with the proper audio and video equipment. I feel the freshest around mid-day, so that is when I like to record all my videos. That way I have lots of time to get all the takes done that I need for my LaToyaForever channel before the day ends. You know I have to take breaks to bug my husband up in his office. Can't have him forgetting he has a wife.

I also take breaks to feed and tend to Zayn. It's so cute how fascinated he is by the whole filming process. He just plays in his area and watches me and the crew do our thing. Sometimes his facial expressions just make me bust out laughing, and I have to stop recording and take a moment. Sometimes he sits

right on my lap, and he helps me respond to comments. If you ever received a comment with a bunch of gibberish, it was most likely from Zayn. Zayn also loves snapchat he's so obsessed with the dog filter, he just smiles and laughs whenever I turn it on. But I wouldn't have it any other way. I love that I can have my son with me while I do my job, it's the best of two worlds.

Meetings and Interviews are typically dispersed throughout the day. I try not to schedule any meetings before 12:30 or after 4:00 pm. It's become more and more difficult as my brand continues to grow and I have to keep the different time zones in mind. But I find if I don't create structure and balance in my life I become a workaholic. I would never want my husband or my kids to think that I put my job or anything else before them. That is one of the things I love about being a YouTube personality, is the flexibility to schedule my day around what is important to my family and even my friends.

Some of my meetings take place over Skype or via telephone. Otherwise, I spend a part of my day driving around the city and meeting up with brands and other YouTubers for possible collaboration ideas.

During my day, I try and fit in some me time wherever possible. I believe that you always have to put your best foot forward no matter how you feel. Since I had my son Zayn, I have been trying to fit the gym into my schedule at least two days per week. I have to keep that waistline looking snatched! I also like to switch things up on a regular basis when it comes to my fashion choices, hair nails, etc. I may go from being a blonde to a redhead in the same week! Girls don't under estimate the power of a healthy makeover. Whenever I am feeling down or just want a pick me up, I find that mixing up my look gives me inspiration and a boost of confidence at the same time.

Throughout my day I meet fans while I am out. It is one of the most enjoyable parts of my day. It is so cool to see all the different types of people that look up to me. To know I bring people together of different ages, races, and cultures is just mind-blowing. It always makes me laugh when I am doing something regular like grocery shopping or buying tampons, and my fans are shocked that they've run into me. Like shoot, do you want to be my assistant? Who do you think does the shopping for my family? I've been told a couple of time that I should get a personal assistant. But then I watch movies like, Fatal Attraction, Obsession, or the newest movie When the Bough Breaks. All of you know I would not stand for having some hot little thing around my family trying to take my place. I like doing everyday things for my family, it keeps me humble. Plus it's easier to hide my crazy purchases from Adam that way!

Adam handles the business side of my online career. I love that we are partners in both life and business. To me, it just means that we bond on so many different levels. In fact, I want to make his title official, but cannot think of an appropriate moniker, musband? Managand? Husbanager? Whatever his title is, Adam is one of the driving forces behind both LaToyaForever and LaToyasLife. I cannot tell you how many times I have come up with something crazy and fun, and Adam tones it down to the more accessible and related version that you all see. He is the yin to my yang. Having that perfect partnership has really helped my brand reach new heights. I love that he isn't afraid to let me take risks. The balance of giving and take in our marriage extends to our business relationship.

Normally when I am out at my meetings, it is time to pick up Samia from her daycare. A lot of people ask me why I don't keep Samia with me all day since I am technically a work-from-home mom. I think it is the superb idea for children to socialize with their peers at a young age. It helps them develop motor skills, cognitive skills, and general people interaction skills. I noticed before, when Samia was with me she was a very solitary child,

and content to be alone rather than surrounded by people. Now that she attends regular daycare, she is a lot more social and outgoing. Honestly, daycare is the best outlet for her. I think it will make the transition to school a lot easier too since she is already established a routine.

Adam schedules any meetings or business of his day around picking up Samia from daycare. He makes sure to get her home, and into her house clothes so she can play outside; her favorite place to be. Sometimes Auntie Jillian picks up Samia from daycare and has her for the remainder of the later afternoon. She loves to go to the park, so my Grandma also takes her there.

The evenings in the Ali house are family time (and sometimes friends too). Most of my friends have full-time jobs or school, so the evenings are when they come to visit my family and me. We watch movies, go to the park, or have dinner together. I grew up with family/friend time centered on meals. So it just seems like I have carried that tradition into my own family life.

One thing I know we lack in our household is having a set family meal time. Our work happens around the clock, and we have to record at random times throughout the day so getting to eat at any time is usually just enough. I do think we need to set in stone some meal time and abide by it. I'll work on it!

I cannot wait until my kids are eating the same things. Right now there are a number of different meals I have to prepare. Zayn is still on the bottle, Samia is thankfully eating solid foods, and Adam likes to eat very healthily, no sodium, low carb meals. I am all about my curry chicken and rice or better yet sushi.

LaToya's Life Uncut mishaps of a youtube star

Lately, I have been on a health kick, trying to keep my waist snatched hunty! Moms of toddlers and young children know how it is, kids eat first. And by eat, I mean, half in the mouth, half all over the house! Once I make sure my kids are fed, Adam and I sit down and eat to talk about our days and anything that has to do with the kids that the other missed.

And then there is bedtime. Adam and I try to make sure Samia is in bed around 8 pm. I normally take Samia up to have her bath around 7:45. It gives her some playtime in the tub, and I can relax for a few, and have some mother-daughter time. We sing songs and bond as Samia tells me about her day. I don't understand it all, but don't worry Samia, mommy is listening.

While Samia and I are having girl time, Adam and Zayn are doing their manly thing!

I have found them doing the craziest things! I love how silly Adam is with our kids. He is so serious normally in our business life, so I love when he brings out the playful side. For example, Adam has a funny video segment on Instagram with Zayn where he dresses him in a Ranger hat. He calls him 'Ranger Zayn' and people seem these short mini-video clips quite entertaining.

Once the kids are put down for the night, Adam and I release whatever videos are needing to go out. While we wait for the videos to upload, I usually try and do some cleaning around the house, or if I have friends over I chill with them for a bit and catch up on all the latest. My friends' have crazy lives, so I just have to try and keep up! Once a video is up, I stay up for a few hours to interact with fans. I feel like that nightly commenting is like an eBook club. We've all watched the same video, and now we are just venting or putting in our two cents about what we think. I feel like on my LaToyasLife vlogs, the comments from the viewers gives my friends, family and I some perspective.

A situation we thought was a big deal, doesn't end up to be even noticed on a vlog, or something we thought was a small thing ends up getting blown out of proportion because of a couple of comments. The comment rebuttals I read sometimes get me laughing out loud for real. Keep up the funny comments Hunty and Huncles!!

At this point in the night, Adam and I talk about what the next day will bring for our schedules. We try and fit some time for us at the end of the day. I find that this is the hardest thing for us to do. By the end of the day, we are both exhausted. But I think it is important for married couples to spend a little bit of each day together. I would never want days to go by without me checking in with my husband; our daily updates help us to continue to grow both together and as a family. Once we complete our daily-tasks it's time for bed, and you'll be surprised by what time it usually is by now...anywhere between 10:30pm-1:00 am).

I hope you all enjoyed a day in the life of me.

Conclusion

'm in awe that I sat my ass down and wrote a book. I'm shocked as I type out this conclusion page. You believed in me and stayed to this point. Writing a book was a lot harder than I thought it would be. It's actually a lot like being on YouTube. In the beginning, it's a struggle to know how much of yourself to put out there and how much to give other people. Then you write draft after draft, getting input and edits that just make you feel like: Am I capable of doing this? Am I supposed to be a writer? Am I expected to tell my story in hopes that it inspires others? Shoot, maybe I am just the funny, wacky girl and I have nothing to say that people will consider important or valuable. Then, slowly, everything starts coming together and you see your vision become a reality. That vision coming to play is the real validation I needed to keep pushing until you have the final product. I learned so much about myself writing this book. I really can do anything I set my mind to.

Through crying babies and sore nipples, I buckled down and got my story out there. And I enjoyed writing the more I got into it. I had thought writing would be a chore. I am not one for sitting in a place for very long. But once I sat down to my computer, the story just flowed out of me. I hope that my story inspires others to follow their dreams and be themselves. As I write this, I think to myself: someone is going to read this, which is a blessing in itself. If it manages to touch a life, well, that would be the cherry on top of my giant sundae. Whether you are a Hunty or a Huncle or just a book-worm who stumbled into this book, I thank you for spending these nine chapters on this journey with me. There were ups and downs, and some things I wasn't sure would play out on paper, but overall, I am grateful. I am grateful to my family and friends for their input on my book, for my editing team for putting up with my crazy behind, and for you for taking a chance in this book.

I kindly invite you to keep up with me on my YouTube channels

My Vlog Life:
YouTube.com/LaToyasLife

My Skits/Beauty/Lifestyle:
YouTube.com/LaToyaforever

I feel compelled to share some wisdom that I have learned with you so that you can soon look back and achieve some things that are meaningful for you. I hope at least one of these insights becomes something you can adopt.

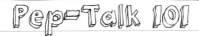

Pep-Talk 101

1. No one really has it figured out in the beginning. All you do is chip away at your goal & adjust accordingly every day. Just move the needle every day!

2. Your WHY truly needs to make you cry. If what you are chasing doesn't get you motivated, then you could be chasing the wrong thing. Focus on your WHY!

3. Count your blessings. It's so easy to play the comparison game in life. Count the blessings because you have a lot to be thankful for.

4. Don't get complacent. Keep dreaming, keep trying new things, stay creative, & network more.

5. Research a lot. Stay informed. You have to keep up with what's going on in this & the ever-changing world we live in. Stay alert so you can get ahead!

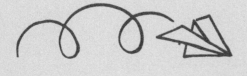

#asklatoya

#AskLaToya

Mel McDuffus asked: Coming from London, I'm curious how hard is it to be a full-time mom, wife, vlogger and still balance your happiness and inner peace?

Hey Mel, so awesome that you're from London. I love London. I've been there two times and hope to go back ten more times, ha-ha. Being a full-time mom, wife, and vlogger is a lot of work, but I truly enjoy every role. Since my life's so hectic, it's so important for me to schedule everything. I love setting goals for myself, and goal setting keeps me organized and sane. It feels so great accomplishing and checking goals off of my list. I use a To Do List app called ERRANDS. It's so cool because I can set alarms to remind me about my tasks that I need to complete for the day. Right now on my work to do list you'll find tasks like: write my business plan, answer questions from supporters, and record main channel video. On my personal to do list is, I have tasks that include: plan the family vacation to Dubai, enroll Samia in dance, and get my nails done. It's important for me

to have a to-do list and check them off as I complete the task. So the key to my happiness and inner peace is to make sure that I set goals and accomplish these goals.

 Danielle McGee asked: First of all, I love you and your amazing friends and family. My question is what is the most memorable moment in your life that you will always remember and why is it special to you?

Hi Danielle, thank you so much, I really appreciate that. I don't have one specific memorable moment, and I can't just pick one, as much as I'd like to. The most memorable year for me was 2014. As you know, I moved to LA to chase my dreams and collaborate with other YouTubers. I then found out I was pregnant with Samia. After finding out I was pregnant Adam and I moved back to Toronto. Right after the move Adam and I flew out to New York where he proposed to me in the middle of Time Square. We then bought a house by the end of the year. We vlogged our entire experience and shared it with the world. I was full of so many emotions that year. I was scared, nervous, overwhelmed, happy, and sad but through it all, I was full of joy. I wanted to share that time with the world, and my supporters which are a big reason why I was able to get through my pregnancy in one piece. Thank you so much.

Nasha Joy asked: I just wanted to say I love you #1FAN, and please have your next meet up in Brooklyn. Also, can you share your wisdom & advice on the best way to start up a successful channel on YouTube? I haven't had much luck in the past and I feel I've might have deleted my video's way too soon.

 What's up Nasha? Brooklyn STAND UP! I will have a meet and greet in New York soon...wait for it. The best advice I can give you when it comes to starting a successful channel is to take one year out of your life and be consistent on YouTube. Research what kind of videos do well in your niche. Do you like beauty videos? Well, what kind of videos are trending in the community? Beauty challenges? Story times? How to put your weave on the right way? Testing out insane beauty hacks? It takes research, a lot of research. Learn how to title your videos, write a good description and how to tag your videos so they rank on the first few pages of YouTube. Also, be active on other platforms on a daily basis. Aside from YouTube I really love using Snapchat and Instagram. Since YouTube is my money maker, I always redirect traffic from other platforms I use back to my YouTube channels. Nasha, a lot of people think that there's a secret way to get instant success on YouTube but there's not. The secret to success is consistency and hard work. Do not focus on the views focus on creating good content and the views will follow. Hope that helped HUNTY :)

Jenai Hollingsworth asked: Whatever happened to the girl that Adam was training that was supposed to make you a dress?

 Hi Jenai, ok so girl I don't know what happened to the girl that Adam used to train? What I do know is after the dress situation we kind of drifted away...slowly. She did make a dress for me but I honestly did not like the dress. The dress would have been good for someone not pregnant, and it was too revealing for my pregnant self. A custom dress would have been great to have but we were cutting it close because my baby shower was the next week and I didn't want to wear something I wasn't comfortable in, so I passed. I went to La Chateau and found a really pretty lace dress that I absolutely loved. I wish her all the best, she's super talented.

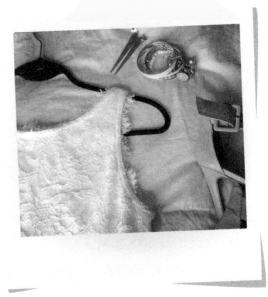

118

Melanie Lewis asked: What did Adam think when you told him you were pregnant with Zayn?

 Hey Mel, so, girl, we were both super shocked. I did not expect to have another baby so fast. When I saw that the pregnancy stick said positive my heart instantly sunk, my entire body got sweaty, and I was overwhelmed with anxiety. When I informed Adam that we were expecting another baby, he was devastated. He always said that he only wanted one baby. Before we found out I was pregnant with Zayn, Adam and I were going through a lot of personal issues in our marriage. So seeing a positive result on that stick wasn't something to jump for joy about. I wasn't too happy, but I was bringing my child into the world and of course when time went on we overcame our personal issues and embraced our beautiful bundle of joy. Zayn completed our family and Adam, and I are in a great place, I'm more in love than ever before.

 Samaya Ali asked: Do you plan on teaching Samia and Zayn (Trini/Somali-Swahili)?

 Hi Samaya! Loving your name girl. It's so close to Samia's name. Anyways, to answer your question. Samia speaks Trini already; it's the funniest thing ever. Trini isn't a language, it's a Caribbean Island, and we speak English with a twist, ha-ha. Let me teach you. If you watch my vlogs, you probably wondering what some of the Trini words mean I use frequently. So a lot of the time I say "A A" which means excuse me. You would say "A A" if you didn't expect something for example if Samia said "MOMMY STOP IT" my response would be "A A." How are you is "Waz de Scene" In Trini. I'm always saying the Trini word "Allyuh" which means you all. So let's say I call up Auntie Jillian, and I say "Auntie allyuh coming

ova," simple right? Would love for you to tweet me and use "A A" and "Allyuh" in a funny sentence ha-ha.

Adam doesn't know how to speak Somali, he knows a few words, but that's about it. So, I don't think the kids will learn Somali. Adam speaks Swahili fluently, and I know how to say a few words. I speak to his mom every other day and every time she says something in Swahili I go to Google and translate from Swahili to English, so I'm learning. We will teach Samia and Zayn how to speak Swahili because when we go to Tanzania, we want them to know how to communicate with their family.

 Ramonna Bishundeo asked: How do you stay positive when you're feeling lonely because your friends are busy and also do you ever question your friendship?

 Hey Ramonna, love your name. How I stay positive when I'm feeling lonely is I do things that make me feel happy. In my house, I'm never alone because I have a husband and two kids so there's always someone by my side. When I used to live on my own years back I was always alone, and I really hated it. What I did to distract me from being alone is I would do things that I enjoyed doing. I loved making YouTube videos, talking to my friends online, talking to family on the phone, taking long drives and exploring new things, taking really long walks, working out, cooking and the list goes on. Distract yourself with things that you truly enjoy doing. Ramonna, I think that you should pick up a hobby, so *you're not so focused on what your friends are doing. If they're your true friends, they will make time for you. If you find yourself questioning your friendships you should talk to your friends about how you feel, have a heart to heart sit down with your friends and just be honest about how you feel. If they're your true friends, they will make changes if not then move on.*

Wileisha Watson asked: I'm in San Francisco and when I watch your videos I wonder how it is that you are always so happy and positive? I love that about you girl.

What's up Wileisha? You're from San Francisco I've been there, super dope city. Anyways, a lot of people think that I'm always positive and happy and funny all the time and girl that's not the case. I'm overall a happy and positive person, but I have times when I want to shut the world out. Example, when I just started YouTube I thought I was a decent looking individual, but then people started to point out the things I was insecure about. They would say things like "oh LaToya your head is so big" and "you have horse teeth" "your boobs are nonexistent." Since those were insecurities of mine, I would be really hurt that people would make fun of me. Now, I embrace my flaws and don't care what people have to say about how I look. Why? Because I'm beautiful inside and out. My flaws make me who I am, and I am unique baby! (HAIR FLIP). Embrace your flaws and remember we are not carbon copies of what people think beautiful should be. We are all beautiful in our own way. I think I just rambled on. Did I answer your question ha-ha? Wileisha, just try your best every day to be happy and do things that you truly enjoy doing, that will help you to stay happy and positive. True happiness starts from within just be happy.

Allia Roberts Guoorah asked: Hi LaToya, coming to you from Trinidad and Tobago! Are you guys planning on having more kids? If no why?

 Hey Allia, Trinidad, jump up girl! Girl, as of right now I don't want any more children. I don't know what the future holds for our family but right now no more kids. We have the best of both worlds, one girl one boy, it's perfect. I don't want to say that I'm never going to have anymore kids because the first two were unplanned. As of right now we are giving all of our love to our two beautiful babies, Samia and Zayn.

 Mathu Kumar asked: Would you ever buy Samia, a puppy?

 What's popping Mathu? Anyways, I'm not an animal person. I think Wawa, our fish is the closest thing Samia will get to having a pet. Plus, Samia's not into dogs. Whenever I take her on walks, and we see a dog she squeezes my legs really tight, screams, begs me to pick her up, or she just takes off running. I just hope to God Samia doesn't want a dog when she's older, pray for me.

Annie Love Pagan asked: What kind of wedding do you want and what role with you kids play in it?

HAY Annie, Adam and I are married, but I really want a wedding. I want an all-white wedding. I want all the decor to be white, and I want all my family and friends to be in white. I want my wedding to feel like I'm getting married in heaven. I want the alter to have white flowers all around it. I want white rose peddles all over the floor. I want an all-white lace dress with a deep Queen Anne neckline. I want my wedding dress train to be 20 feet long, is that possible, ha-ha? With Zayn and Samia positioned on the train as I walk down. The impossible will be possible on my wedding day. I'd be such a bridezilla. I so need to document the process of planning my wedding, can we say hot mess?

Natalie Owusu-ansah asked: If you could pick a country to travel to and stay there for a year, what would you pick?

Hey Hunty Natalie, I think that I would travel to Dubai and stay there for a year. Dubai is breathtaking, period. The architecture is so beautifully designed, and the skylines are something you only see in pictures and on TV. The Burj Khalifa is the coolest building and the highest building I've ever seen in real life. I think it's the tallest building in the world. I felt like a speck of dust standing next to it, and I don't think I'll ever go to the top it's just too high, but it's great to look at. When I visited Dubai in 2015 I did not want to leave, the shopping, the diversity, the luxury, the food, the beaches, the views, the beautiful fountains...it was amazing. I'm actually planning a family trip to Dubai soon.

Mayumi Robyn Maeda asked: Here in Tokyo, I always wonder how you slay in your selfie game?

 Hey Mayumi, Tokyo stand up! I've been to Japan a few times. My dad played professional baseball in Tokyo, Japan. Anyways, how I slay my selfies is a beat face, a ring light, or natural lighting and my signature pose. I also use a few editing apps. I use face tune, snapseed, and VSCO. These apps really help enhance my pictures. I use face tune to smooth out my skin sometimes, I also whiten my teeth, and my eyeballs. If my edges are not laid well I use the smooth tool to lay them, bad boys, down! I use VSCO for the filters. They have the best filters in my opinion. I use this filter called S1, and it's so bombs, I use that filter on all of my pictures.

For my Outfit of the Day posts, I make sure I slay my outfits at all time. I love bodycon dresses, jumpsuits, crop tops, high-waist jeans, flannel shirt wrapped around my waist, baseball cap sometimes, and long weave. I get a lot of my fashion inspiration from Kim Kardashian as I'm so obsessed with her style. Some online stores I love to shop at are Hot Miami Styles, Ha-haa Shoetique, Go Jane, and Ego Official are the first ones that come to mind. Hope that was helpful. Keep on slaying!

Isabelle Izzy asked: Do you regret anything in your life?

 I don't want to say I regret anything in my life because the choices I've made in my past is the reason why I'm here today. I've overcome all of the stupid things I've done in my life, and I look at it as lessons learned. So no I don't regret anything I've done and if I had the opportunity to go back in time and change things I would leave it the same because I'm so happy. I love my life! Those past mistakes are the reason why I work so hard today. :)

Uncut Mishaps

Behind the Scene Stories from Friends and Family

From Auntie Jillian

I t wasn't easy for a baby to come into the world having teenage parents. But when our family was blessed with LaToya, it was like she had been here all along. The family took over making sure that she didn't want for anything. If there is a word such as "over-spoiled," then that's what we did to LaToya. She was like our prized possession, and we treated her like one.

We've had endless funny moments with her from when she was a baby all the way to a grown lady. If I were to pick one, I would choose when she made me laugh so hard in the water while vacationing in Tobago. I thought we were both going to drown because she saw a tiny fish in the water. She panicked while holding onto me, and she pulled us under the water where we both struggled. The water was probably only shoulder high for me, so we had a good laugh. We also used to laugh because she said that she wanted to change her name from "LaToya" to something plain.

She said it was because an employer would know she was black and may not hire here before seeing her. She said her name doesn't look good on a resume.

There have been so many crazy moments with LaToya that I call her **"Queen Crazy!"**

From Cousin Ana

When LaToya's grandma first moved into her house, she specifically told LaToya, Myles and I not to eat any food on the carpet. Of course, as kids, you could not tell us that. So we would always sneak food in. One day, she made soup for us and Myles had to be a little shit disturber. He decided to ruin it for all of us, and he walked out of the kitchen and spilled soup all over the brand new beige carpet! Auntie Janice was so pissed that she could not even get the words out, and started yelling at him in basically gibberish, since none of us could understand her. Stunned, Myles just stood there while LaToya and I laughed until we cried and couldn't breathe. Eventually, we all snapped out of it and helped Myles clean up the mess.

It used to be tradition that LaToya and I would spend Christmas night together so that we could go Boxing Day shopping. One Christmas we came back to my house tipsy, and LaToya started singing an old Trinidadian Parang (Calypso Christmas Carols) song. Part of the lyrics say: "I want a piece of pork for Christmas." LaToya promptly turns to me and says: *"Ana, why is he singing about pork? Don't people have turkeys for Christmas?"* So then I say to her: *"in Trinidad, they usually have a Christmas ham instead."* Confused, she then says: *"they have the animal ham for Christmas?"* So I look at her and say: *"huh? What did you say?"* And she says: *"you know the animal ham?"*

At this point, I'm dead from laughing. I'm crying laughing, and she starts to laugh too. We laugh so much so that I fell off my bed onto the floor. Hearing this, my sister comes in the room. We explain the whole story to her, and she rolls her eyes and looks at us and says: **"you two are crazy."** After we compose ourselves, I told LaToya that ham comes from a pig; it's pork! We still relive the telling of this story today and laugh till we cry.

From Cousin Myles

The moment that sticks out in my mind the most comes from our childhood days when LaToya and I would go to church with our grandmother. This was a normal thing because our grandmother is religious and has been going to the same Roman Catholic Church since her immigration to Canada from Trinidad. All of our family has had experiences in this church: weddings, baptisms, communions, confirmations, etc. Of course, LaToya was not present for all of them due to her moving around as a child. However, during a time when she was living in Toronto, LaToya, my grandma and I went to church, LaToya brought us back some of her other church experiences from the States.

When we got home from church one particular day, we were telling our grandma how boring the service was and how happy we were to be home. The way I remember this was literally like a YouTube skit (and this was years before YouTube existed). Another thing that LaToya and I constantly laugh at each other about is our singing voices. We just happened to end up comparing the hymns in the Roman Catholic Church—which are usually slow to medium tempo—to the hymns in American Baptist Churches (which are usually high tempo and exciting to be around).

I've only seen recreations of these churches on televisions and in movies, but she had real experiences of them, which I found to be hilarious because her imitations of them seemed so real. We started to sing the slow songs and act out people's mannerisms while singing the songs. Then, we sang the upbeat songs and jumped and sang very loud. LaToya acted out how churchgoers would speak in tongues, and it was all very funny to us! But our grandma got annoyed and told us to stop. This was definitely a great memory for us, and we still talk about it to this day.

The craziest most recent memory I've shared with LaToya was definitely the Range Rover Incident. For everybody who watches the vlogs, you should be familiar with the time that PJ took the Range Rover to film a video for himself. I was there for the beginning of the video shoot, enjoying the music and company of friends and family, and made a quick appearance in the video. Then, I went to our neighbour's child's birthday party. LaToya was there with Samia, along with more family, so I was there hanging out and talking to everybody. As I was there, I was getting a lot of missed calls from the people who were at the video shoot. I was in a basement with a bad connection, so I didn't answer. Then all of a sudden, I was in mid-conversation with LaToya and some other family when I look down at my phone and see a picture of the Range Rover submerged in mud.

For anybody who knows me, they know I'm normally very calm and collected. But it was very hard for me to keep my calm demeanor after seeing this! I don't remember saying bye to anybody, I just remember leaving and driving towards the shoot because I had to see this with my own eyes. After getting to the scene of the crime, I remember the most terrifying phone call I've ever received from LaToya. She was obviously livid after learning what had happened to her car, and at me for having learned about it while I was in her presence and not mentioning it. Hey, I didn't want to be the one to tell her that her expensive car is stuck in mud! I'll never forget this phone call because although I couldn't understand what she was saying, I knew exactly what the call was about. She cussed me out so badly for about 5 straight minutes and then hung up. This will remain an unforgettable memory for me.

from LaToya's Best Friend, Ayanna

A crazy/odd time i've shared with LaToya was at the end of our high school year, back when Black Planet, Myspace, and all those types of sites were popular and everyone was on it. We decided to create our own together and it somewhat had a **Mean Girls** vibe to it. We called ourselves **"De Plastix"** in reference to the one group of girls in the movie. Ha-ha I know, how weird, but we did. Back then, we got comments saying that we always looked alike/similar or could pass for sisters, so we did just that. We set it, had a full on photoshoot, took it way to seriously and just created the page.

Not for attention or anything, but because it was fun and so so random of us to do at that moment. We just closed her dad's office doors and got to work creating the name, taking pictures, making our "sister" bio. Almost everyday after school, we checked on it and worked on it. It's hilarious to think about it now and have the one main picture to look back on. So young and being in the hype of it all.

After our high school's prom, a small group of us all went up to Montreal for the weekend. We were driven by my mother, and all 6 of us stayed at my aunt's house downtown. On our 1st full day there, we walked the downtown streets and had fun popping into random shops (even ones we shouldn't have been) and stores and enjoying the french culture. But that night, we all decided to go to a club! It was our first time going to one, and since the legal drinking age is 18 in Montreal, we were able to go no problem. We got all dressed up and excited to go, and walking in and seeing the lights, music—the whole 'club atmosphere'—was surreal to us.

We were doing what all the older teens/adults are doing. We danced, scoped out the whole place, saw people getting on wild and acting a fool at times. Just being thrown into the scene, we stuck together. We later walked around, ate street food and joked and laughed about the night and what we experienced. At that age, it was something to remember.

OUTTAKES
Additional Stories
& Alternate Endings

I was approaching the end of high school and as a gift, my Dad agreed to buy me a car. I was very excited, I felt like my luck and situation had finally turned around, but once again I got knocked back down to earth. My dad and I had gone to the Honda dealership. My Dad pointed at a white two door Honda Civic and asked me if I liked it, and I said **"HELL YES I LOVE IT"** my dad smiled and said "Ok" and he said we would get it. The very next day my Dad had a change of heart. My Stepmom convinced him not to get me a car because my grades weren't up to her perfect standards. And she also made note that they have to pay for my tuition when I go to college, and how she didn't have a car when she was my age. It's funny because my Dad bought her her first car so why's she preventing me from getting a car.

After high school, I wanted to go to post-secondary school, so I enrolled and got accepted at **York University** for communications. A few months into the program I hated it so much, I was getting poor grades and I just stopped going. I went to school every day but I never went to class I hung out in the cafeteria with friends commenting on Facebook pictures, taking pictures to post on my Facebook wall, had photoshoots with friends around the campus.

I couldn't picture my life doing business administration

I completed my first semester but doing so I realized how little I liked my course, and I had no passion for it. I couldn't see myself pursuing something I had no interest in, so I dropped out.

I felt like more of an outcast at home in Canada than I did in Tulsa. I also really missed my mom, so I once again moved back to Tulsa and enrolled in a community college there for Business Administration. I was eligible to work on campus because I was seen as an international student. Unfortunately, I wasn't happy. I hated what I was studying, and I couldn't picture my life doing business administration. After completing one full year, I decided to drop out. I did a lot of soul-searching and tried to figure out what I wanted to do with my life. I thought about what genuinely interest me, and what naturally excelled in. And it hit me. My passion was in entertainment. Entertaining people made me feel happy, and I was naturally good at it.

Blog TV wasn't making me any money. No lie, I had absolutely no money to my name. I dropped out of school after completing a year and since I left school I couldn't work on campus anymore. I still had the social security number that immigration issued me so I could work on campus, but of course the social security card had stipulations. One of them was I couldn't work off campus without permission. Which was a bummer because I wasn't in school anymore.

Being who I am, I still applied for jobs off campus and I got a call back from a call center, I was so happy! Oh my God, so happy. So I went in and gave them my social security number and they hired me ya'll, I just beat the system and they never found out. I was working at a Bank of America call center after a few months I left. I was in a rut because working at a call center was not what I wanted to do, I wasn't happy with my life, I was bigger than working at a damn call center. I wanted to be in the entertainment industry. I met a guy from online and he said he would help me with a modeling and acting career and how he helped other girls in the industry. He was based out of Dallas TX. I was so down and so excited I was about to finally be in the entertainment industry. So I bought a ticket to Dallas, TX and he picked me up from the airport.

He was telling me all about the modeling agency and how I needed to hire a photographer, get pictures taken for my portfolio, and essentially build an entire brand. He told me that he would start sending me to auditions and go sees and how he would get me into all the magazines, I was so excited. I asked him if I could stay with him for a week so I could get my portfolio done and he said yes. So I stayed with him. A few days went by and he started to make moves on me, I was not having it. I told him no multiple times that night.

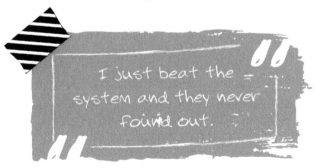

I just beat the system and they never found out.

A few more days went by and he would continue. I slept on the couch every night, I would never flirt with him, I just wanted my modeling career to at least get me into the industry and then I could do other things like get my own shows, start a clothing line, fragrance line something, I knew I had to start somewhere. Ya'll this guy got so aggressive with me he pulled me into his room and said that if I don't have sex with him that I would never make it in the modeling agency and how all the other girls he works with has sex with him and how I'm lucky to even be staying with him and how he usually "pimps bitches" like me out. Ya'll I busted into tears and I don't know what hit me but I kicked him straight in the balls and ran my ass out of his apartment. He ran after me but ya'll I took off ducking and dodging throughout his apartments he was chasing after me but he couldn't keep up with me, ya'll something came over me, God was with me that night. I went straight to the airport and went back to Tulsa. WHAT A WASTE!

"God was with me that night!"

Back in Tulsa, I was doing nothing with my life.

I convinced one of my best friend at the time who wanted to be in the entertainment industry as well that we needed to be in Dallas if we want to make it.

So we picked up and we flew out to Dallas. All I know is thank God for my Dad who sent me money here and there and I had the money that I saved up from my call center job. We had to stay at a motel for some time, we got pictures done, we partied, we met cool people. We were having the time of our life. After about a month, we were running low on money so we had to get jobs. We got our smart serve and we got jobs at a bar. We started making money and I met a guy from the bar I was working at. He was always at the bar getting smashed every single weekend and it was all good with me because he would buy a bottle and then tip me $200. I loved when he came in. Anyway, we became friends and he started buying me things. He bought me a car, he leased an apartment for me for 6 months, he gave me money, and he took me shopping. I was living the life. I quit my job at the bar. You could call him a sugar daddy.

During this time I met a guy from an online website and he lived back in Toronto. We became very serious. We spent all day and night on the phone. I finally told him to fly out to Dallas to see me so we could finally meet each other in person, I really liked him ya'll. Just so you can get a visual he was white, over 6'7, clean fade, he was so tall that whenever we wore jeans they would hit his ankle. Anyway, we got back to my place and he pulled out a teddy bear and flowers and it was the cutest thing ever. Then he said look on the teddy bear and I was so excited to find a ring. And he said it's a promise ring, so sweet. Anyway, D and I got super close. I loved spending time with him. I loved that he was so supportive whenever I talked about my dreams and aspirations. D convinced me to move back to Toronto because nothing was really going on for me in Dallas. I wanted to make a name for myself, but I didn't want to have to depend on a sugar daddy for money. So D and I drove my Toyota Prius to Toronto and the journey back to Toronto was lots of fun. We got back to Toronto and I was going to move in with D at first, but changed my mind. I told my Dad I'm moving in with him, but I was barely at my dad's. I was always with D.

I remember we would be out partying all the time and you know that with partying, alcohol and drugs are involved. Thankfully, I was never into drugs. The only drug I've ever tried was marijuana, but I stopped that quickly after a terrible trip.

D and I used to drink at least 4 times a week. It was super excessive. My Auntie Jillian was convinced D and I had a drinking problem.

I remember auditioning to be a host for **Much Music**....

During this time I was talking to a boy that I had met back in Toronto. We became very serious, and he tried to convince me to move in with him. What he was saying made a lot of sense at the time because I could work there, and I felt like I could start fresh. So I agreed, and I once again moved back to Toronto.

Moving in with him wasn't as glamorous as I had imagined and I still had a burning desire to make videos. Without Blog TV as an option, I decided I had to look to other avenues. I applied to be a host on one of Canada's premiere music television networks, and I went through several rounds of auditions. I was extremely excited because everything seemed to be going so well for me. All of the producers loved me, and I really got my hopes up. But when I didn't get the job, it hit me like a ton of bricks. I went to several other auditions, but I kept receiving rejection after rejection. This was very defeating and made me question if entertainment was really for me.

I remember D writing long letters to the producers of **Much Music** since he was so upset that they had disqualified me. D encouraged me to stay consistent with my **YouTube** channel. While in Dallas, I would create videos on **YouTube,** but I was not consistent because I didn't know exactly what I wanted to do on **YouTube.** I felt like I needed a series of some sort. D and I came up with a series to document of me trying to become a model — getting headshots, finding a photographer, going to go-sees. I did that for about 3 videos and quit because I didn't want to become a model anymore, it wasn't me. I wanted to entertain and I wanted to make people laugh. I remember that one time I spent the entire day at the dad's house filming a

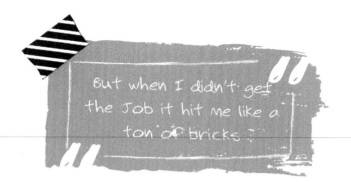

But when I didn't get the Job it hit me like a ton of bricks ="

scene from the **"Mean Girls".** Do you remember the phone call part from the movie? Yes, that scene was trending on **YouTube**, and so all YouTubers were doing it at the time.

I decided to create a video as well, and I played all the characters in the movie. I changed scenes, changed wardrobe, and learned all the times. It took me all day to edit the video. My video got over 20,000 hits and oh my God, I was so excited about that I started to get an explosion of subscribers from that video. You'll never find the video though because my stepmom and dad made me remove the video saying their house was exposed and I never asked for permission, blah-blah. So I put the video on private, and I hope that one day you all will be able to see it. After that disaster, I recorded another video in the backyard doing a bathing suit haul and of course my stepmom and dad made me remove it saying the neighbors complained about it (which was not true). That video got 13K views. They were really preventing me from growing my YouTube brand. I was having so much fun on YouTube and I truly enjoyed what I was doing. Then I had to sneak and create videos. What I would do is whisper while doing videos in my room in front of my door.

Even when I moved away from my family to go to Los Angeles, I had caring people looking out for me. I didn't want to call Adam and tell him on the phone. I wanted to let him know in person. But he had just left and wasn't going to come back for a few days, and there was no way I was going to wait that long. So I called him and let him know he had to get back here ASAP. I wanted him to be there for the first appointment, and all the new milestones we were about to experience. Adam immediately changed his plans to come back and be there with me. Unfortunately, the border patrol didn't want to grant him access back to the United States. For some reason, they were not convinced he was going to be returning. However, after 6 hours of proving all he wanted to do was grab his pregnant lady and his car, they finally let him in with a condition that he would need to return to Canada within a week.

Being pregnant was not at all what I expected. You can never prepare for how much it changes you as a person. I fell in love with Samia from when I saw the first tiny spec on the ultrasound. I may have hated being pregnant, but the result is unparalleled. Being larger and waddling was not my idea of a good time. It was hard to get around and do the things I usually wanted to do. Even when the doctor put me on bed rest, I didn't quite believe that I couldn't just carry on with my life while nurturing my baby. You certainly do have to re-evaluate your priorities when you are expecting.

Looking back now, I truly believe that all of that rejection was an important part of building my character and pushing me to become the person I am today. I got fed up with rejection and decided to start a **YouTube** channel. **YouTube** was relatively new when I adopted it, and those who were on were just like me, looking for a platform to express. The need to express was all I needed, a safe-haven where I could express what I wanted without any limitations. Things with my boyfriend became more and more rocky. I was still very young and I wasn't ready or willing to start a life with him, so we split up. My relationship started to crumble and we would fight about the stupidest things— I remember he accused me of seeing another guy and he said that I was lying because people who lie look to the left. He was so jealous and thought I was up to no good. I barely saw my friends because he was insecure and I didn't want to upset him. Anyway, I had had enough of the jealousy and got sick of the drinking. And we split up and I moved back in with my dad temporarily.

> ❝ I had caring people looking out for me. ❞

My **YouTube** channel began to pick up and my videos were receiving a lot of attention and views. It was during this time that I first thought that maybe I could really do this. Maybe I could go full force into producing content and maybe make a living on YouTube. From that moment I put all of my efforts and energy into pursuing my dream of making it big on **YouTube**, and since then I have never looked back.

> Being pregnant was not at all what I expected. You can never prepare for how much it changes you as a person.

People would say things like I'm a terrible friend, I'm fake, Adam deserves better, I'm ugly without makeup, I'm fat, I'm rude, I have terrible weave, nobody likes you, everyone's using you, just an army of negative Nancys came out of the woodworks to tear me down.

YouTube was still in its infancy; less than five years since creation. One of my earlier videos was in response to questions on if I bleach my skin. As I've grown up, my skin is lighter than it was in my previous videos. I wanted to quash all the haters and the rude questions; I was proud of my skin. When I was a teenager, I would always go tanning with my cousin Ana. I loved the sun-kissed look it gave us; we thought we were a big deal. As I grew older, I learned the dangers of fake tanning and stopped going to the tanning beds. Unfortunately, the reaction to being well-educated on the risks of skin cancer meant that people noticed my skin appeared lighter than they were used to. Some of the negative comments I received were "*I think you're really a crazy white girl that spends too much time under the sunlamps"* another wrote *"you lying s*** you are bleaching! Your mother is black, and your father is too. And my personal favorite 'you're not black'."*

Shortly after getting pregnant with my daughter Samia, I wanted to take a break from my comedy channel to focus on my pregnancy. I wanted to share what I was going through with my viewers. I also felt like I couldn't always be that crazy and fun girl everyone was so used to seeing every week because I didn't always feel happy. When I got pregnant, I was full of different emotions, and I wanted to share those moments with my viewers. When I decided to share my personal life with the world is when a small group of people started to form opinions about who I really was.

People began to judge me and how I lived my life. People would call me a bitch all the time; I was pregnant for heaven sake. Clearly, those jerks haven't been pregnant before. People started forum threads and Instagram pages to "take me down" because they thought I was this evil person. A lot of people put me on a pedestal that I didn't ask to be on. So they attacked and judged me for every move that wasn't in line with their beliefs. Through all the judgment, I was still happy because I was able to express myself and be me. I was able to share that with the world and in life everyone isn't going to agree with you or like you.

Here I was trying to reach out to fans that were questioning my authenticity, my race and these are the types of responses I received. It was then I realized that no matter what I told people they were going to believe what they wanted to believe. It didn't matter if I were authentic or fake, people would draw their conclusions on who they thought I was. That was hard for me to understand in the beginning.

Finding Out I Was Pregnant (Alternate Version)

remember the day I found out I was pregnant, Adam, and I had just moved to LA; we hadn't even been there a couple of months. I was trying to tone up my body and lose some weight that I just couldn't shake. My friend Maya was making fun of me, because no matter how many reps I did, and how often I went to the gym, I wasn't losing any belly weight if anything I was getting flabbier around my midsection. There was one particular day when she was mocking my weak arms and my ever increasing chest. She kept insisting that I must be pregnant or something because the weight I was keeping on didn't make any sense. We left my apartment in Hollywood and went to the drug store to pick up a pregnancy test. I only went to shut her up because I didn't believe her.

Imagine my shock when the stick indicated positive! Adam wasn't even in town at the time. He had flown back to Toronto to deal with some family matters. My friend Maya was there for me while I panicked. I had just picked up my entire life and moved to LA. I had business deals, and brand deals in the works, and was starting to establish myself out there. I had friends, but the majority of my familial support system was back in Toronto. I didn't know what I was supposed to do.

Author Bio

In early 2010, LaToya Ali entered the online social scene capturing the hearts of video viewers from all around the world. LaToya's charisma and incredible wit are among the few traits she is known for when expressing her candid opinions. Born in Scarborough, Ontario, to Trinidadian parents, LaToya is the eldest of eight children. When she was entering middle school her mother decided to pursue a college education in the US. Arriving to the US wasn't such a comfortable experience for LaToya. While continuously having to pack up her bags, she never really had the opportunity to develop strong relationships with friends. With the desire to express her feelings, LaToya picked up a digital camera and began recording an open-diary video series on YouTube. Presently, LaToya has nearly 1,600,000+ subscribers combining 2 of her YouTube channels and the exclusive access to a captivated audience has provided her with numerous career opportunities, such as media appearances both in print and on screen. In November 2012, LaToya was announced as a host for *VIBE TV* at the *American Music Awards*. As *VIBE* host she interviewed a number of stars, including J Cole. During this role she questioned J Cole about his album **"Born Sinner".** At the same award shows she interviewed Destorm Power.

Acknowledgements

First and foremost, thank you God, thank you for today, yesterday and tomorrow. My family, my joys, my sorrows. For all that made me stronger. I would like to express my sincere appreciation to all my supporters around the world. Whether you bought this book or not thank you for taking the time to read this. Thank you for seeing something in me through my work online. My Huntys and Huncles are my extended family, and I do not say that lightly.

I would like to express my appreciation to all my family members who provided support, shared stories, remarks, and gave me the opportunity to go through memory lane with you. I cherished those moments.

Thank you, mom. I love you.

I would like to thank Mango Publishing for seeing value in what I do and being persistent in getting me to share my story through these pages. It forced me to tap into skillsets I never knew I had. It also put me in a position to challenge myself and to develop the discipline that I am sure will crossover to the many more chapters of my life.

Krystle Wiltshire was very accessible anytime I needed to bounce ideas or simple finding great words to help me get my point across. This book would not be possible without you. Thank you so much!

Special thanks to my husband Adam for being on my tail almost every day and being the casting support I needed to get this project done.

To my children Samia and Zayn, everything I do is for you. I trust you to uphold our family to your best abilities and always remember that family is the best thing in this life to hold on to.

Lastly, please forgive me sincerely for all those that walked this journey with me thus far and that I have not mentioned here. You remain in my heart cherished forever.

- LaToya Forever

CPSIA information can be obtained
at www.ICGtesting.com
Printed in the USA
BVOW11s1637161016
465116BV00004B/4/P